9.75

CYPRUS
THE UNFINISHED AGONY

This book I dedicate to the memory of my beloved parents who have lived and died as true and faithful citizens of Cyprus.

CYPRUS
THE UNFINISHED AGONY

Dr P. N. Vanezis

Abelard-Schuman
London

By the same author:

Makarios: Faith and Power
Makarios: Pragmatism v. Idealism

© 1977 P. N. Vanezis
First published by Abelard-Schuman Limited 1977

ISBN

All rights reserved. No part of this publication may be reproduced, stored in a retrieval system, or transmitted in any form or by any means, electronic, mechanical, photocopying, recording or otherwise, without the written permission of the publisher.

Abelard-Schuman Limited
450 Edgware Road
London W2 1EG

Reproduced and printed by photolithography and bound in Great Britain at The Pitman Press, Bath

Contents

Acknowledgements	vii
Introduction	1

PART A

I	The Birth of the Republic	7
II	The Years of Adjustment	18
III	Intercommunal Friction	30

PART B

IV	The Greek Coup and its Repercussions on Cyprus	43
V	International Power Politics and Cyprus	51
VI	The Invasion and Drama of Cyprus	58

PART C

VII	Economic, Social and Political Consequences	73
VIII	Solution or Dissolution	82
IX	Analysis of the most recent events	90
X	Conclusion—Prospects	99

Notes	105
Bibliography	112
Appendices	116

Acknowledgements

The author would like to sincerely thank the many Greek and Turkish, political and non-political, Cypriots, and his British friends whose valuable assistance and constructive criticism have helped to complete this book.

The author would also like to thank his wife for her help and for her patience in tolerating the upset of household and social activities for the sake of his literary efforts.

Finally the author would like to point out that all the views expressed in this book are entirely his own and in no way commit the Government of the Republic of Cyprus which he serves.

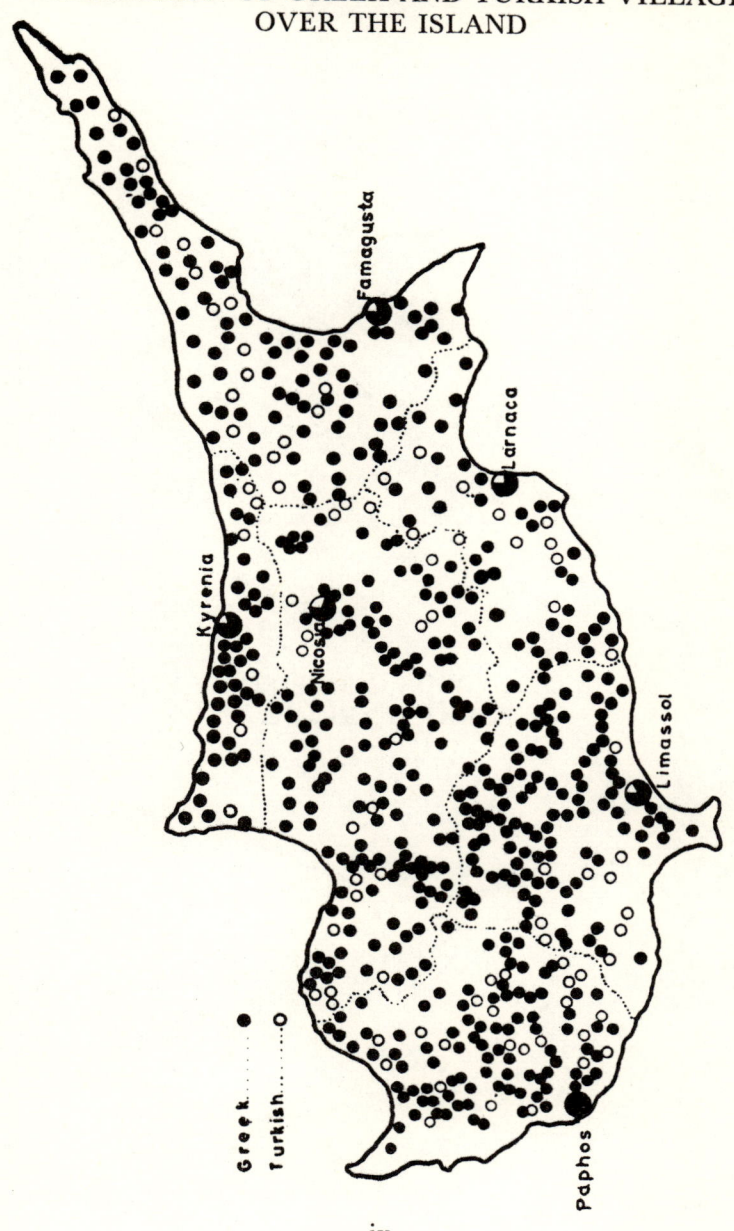

LAND OWNERSHIP IN CYPRUS

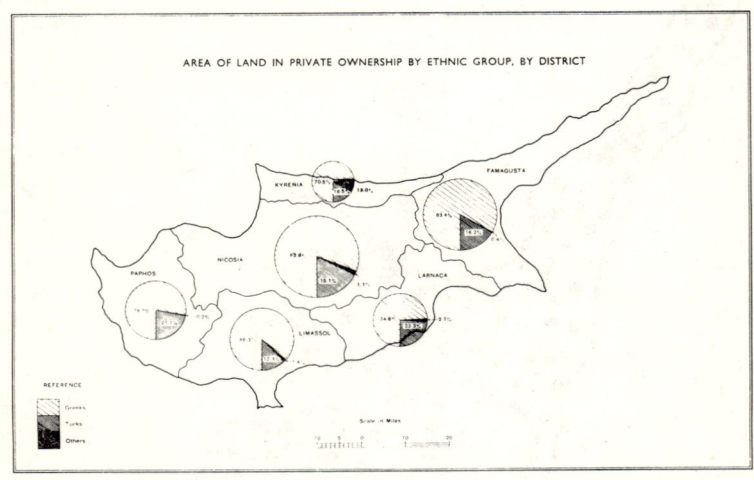

AREA OF CYPRUS OCCUPIED BY THE TURKISH TROOPS

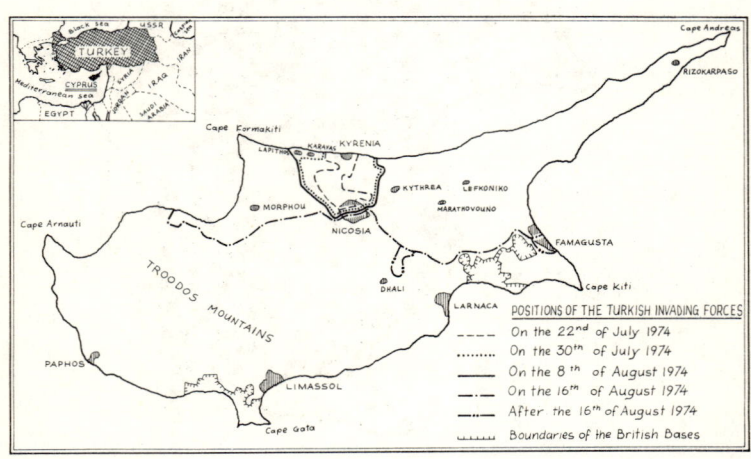

Introduction

Ever since the Turkish minority had access to arms in December 1963, and prevented the political development of the Republic, there has been armed violence in Cyprus. In July 1974, this course of violence reached its peak first with the armed coup engineered by the Greek military junta of Athens against President Makarios on 15th July 1974, and then with the Turkish invasion and seizure of 40 percent of the island. It seemed as if Turkish military intervention would trigger off war between Greece and Turkey. However, in Greece the fall of the military dictatorship has, so far, prevented the development of a full scale Graeco-Turkish conflict; but if the problem of invaded Cyprus remains unresolved, there is the possibility of such a conflict breaking out in the near future. This would be catastrophic for N.A.T.O., would bring war to the Eastern Mediterranean, and could have graver consequences.

United Nations troops have been in Cyprus (UNFICYP) since 1964 to provide a buffer between the two communities, but not to prevent armed conflict by a much stronger power. It is, therefore, in the interests of the major powers acting in concert, if necessary outside the U.N., to strive for a speedy, effective and just solution of the problems of the island before they deteriorate, to the point of no return.

The most distasteful feature of the Turkish rape of Cyprus had been its hypocrisy and political inconsistency. The Turkish Government of July 1974, headed by Mr. B. Ecevit, wanted to take military action in Cyprus under the tripartite Treaty. The three guarantors were Britain, Greece and Turkey. At that time, though, Greece was not considered a reliable guarantor because of the coup against Archbishop Makarios. Nevertheless, Mr. Ecevit approached Britain to act jointly with Turkey under the Treaty of Guarantee to restore the legitimate Government of the Republic of Cyprus. Had Britain fulfilled her treaty obligations the worst aspects of the Cypriot tragedy would have been avoided. This inability of Britain to act decisively is most unfortunate. Britain refused to act under the Treaty of Guarantee against the coup in Cyprus on the grounds that any changes in the personnel of the Government of Cyprus were not covered by the Treaty.[1] This left Turkey a free hand to act unilaterally. Turkey wanted a full scale invasion of the island, declaring that her sole objective was the fulfilment of her treaty obligations and the restoration of the Government of Archbishop Makarios. No sooner, however, had the Turkish army established itself in Cyprus, then the real plans of the Turkish Government were revealed. They conquered almost 40 percent of the island, expelling the Greek Cypriots and declaring this area Turkish territory. It was either to be an exclusive zone of Cyprus, or to be annexed by Turkey. This two-faced attitude on the part of Turkey could either have been the result of a long premeditated ambition, or else their initial military success tempted them to conquer further.

The Turkish invasion of Cyprus, and the seizure of 40 percent of the island by force is a direct affront to the conscience of the whole world. The existence of the U.N. Charter has proved totally inadequate to serve the purposes for which it has been intended.

The Cypriots outlook is influenced too much by religious and racial-ethnic differences and this has aggravated conflict between the Greek and Turkish communities. The Greek Cypriots have overlooked this in their singleminded pursuit of 'enosis and only enosis'. The majority of the Greek Cypriots, until it was too late, hardly ever gave a serious thought to compromising with their Turkish co-citizens. Too many Greek Cypriots did not mind confronting the Turks in the name of the 'Megale Idea'. The Turkish Cypriots, on the other hand, would never forget that they were the former masters of the island, and continued to claim, despite their inferior numbers, political equality with the Greek Cypriots. The two attitudes can be best summed up as the pride of the Greek Cypriot and the unjust obstruction of the Turkish Cypriots.

The situation which Turkey is striving to create in Cyprus closely resembles the Irish problem. The native population has been driven from a part of the island, and their lands have been seized. The intention is to have only Turks in the occupied area, thus creating another Ulster within Cyprus. This analogy will become a homology if the partition of Cyprus results in the Turkish section being linked with Turkey. A 'Republic of Turkey and Northern Cyprus' will create endless trouble because the expelled population will strike back eventually.

The author hopes that by honestly presenting the problem, he will contribute to its solution by promoting an understanding of the situation. In addition, the author proposes various means of providing Cyprus with an adequate political and constitutional structure to satisfy its bi-racial character and to secure its independence, unity, integrity and neutrality. Partition must inevitably lead to the Turkish annexation of the Turkish Cypriot area. The exclusive allegiance of all Cypriots should be to the Cypriot flag, and to a National Anthem. Very often, minor things such as these help to foster national unity.

In conclusion, it is hoped that the tragic events of 1974 might have served a useful purpose by eliminating certain features which were hindering the settlement of the Cyprus problem. The price paid has, no doubt, been too high, but let us hope that the lesson learned by all will prove to be invaluable.

PART A

I
The Birth of the Republic

Cyprus, the third[1] largest island (after Sicily and Sardina) in the Mediterranean, has enjoyed a pre-eminent and unique position in the history of colonialism[2] by having been part of two decaying empires—the Ottoman and the British. In fact, from 1878-1914, Cyprus established a record of being simultaneously a part of both. This came about through the occupation of Cyprus by Britain in 1878[3] when Cyprus became a British military base, while legally remaining Ottoman territory. The present problem is the result of the decay of these two empires. The passage of these two empires through history has left behind ruins and confusion which have caused untold suffering to mankind.

The establishment of the British presence in Cyprus in 1878 coincided with the desire of the Greek Cypriots to be united with the independent Greek nation. Britain, the nation of Byron and Canning, inspired such a hope both in Cyprus and in Greece. World War I ended all Turkish sovereignty over Cyprus[4] and brought about a renewed enthusiasm for union with Greece (Enosis). Britain continued to rule Cyprus under a colonial regime, relying more and more upon the Turkish minority (18 percent of the population) to police and administer the island.

After the end of World War II, Cyprus, like Indo-China and French North Africa, became one of the focal points of the struggle against colonialism. An extremely efficient underground organization known as E.O.K.A.[5] started an armed struggle against the British colonial administration in 1955. The struggle was waged with ruthlessness and ferocity, and Britain in order to maintain her position, had to rely more and more on the Turkish minority and encouraged the same minority to oppose the claim of the Greek majority to national self-determination. The British sought to counter the Greek hopes by bringing Turkey into the picture and giving the Republic of Turkey rights in Cyprus which they had signed away at Lausanne in 1923. The British Government, as the sovereign power, was entitled to reintroduce Turkey into Cyprus. The Turkish opposition to the Greek Cypriots inspired by Britain, resulted in a virtual civil war in Cyprus, and, outside Cyprus, in a confrontation between Greece and Turkey. In the end, this British policy succeeded in blocking the union of the island with Greece, but made the continuation of British rule impossible.

The so-called Cyprus settlement of 1959/60 was unsatisfactory. The British Government encouraged Greece and Turkey (both allies of Britain in N.A.T.O.) to reach a compromise over Cyprus by which Cyprus was declared to be a sovereign Republic with both parties retaining considerable rights in it. The same sovereign Republic of Cyprus, chose to remain a member of the British Commonwealth. The intricacy and the illogicality of such political and diplomatic acrobatics are an insult to both intelligence and morality. Britain then joined Greece and Turkey in forcing[6] Archbishop Makarios, the Greek Cypriot leader, to accept this Treaty and a Constitution based on it.

The birth of the Republic of Cyprus took place in London between February 17th and 19th, 1959, at Lancaster House. These were the dates of the London/Cyprus Conference attended by the Prime Ministers and Foreign Ministers of Britain, Greece and Turkey as well as Archbishop Makarios and Dr. F. Kuchuk representing the Greek and Turkish communities of Cyprus respectively. The American Greek author, Stephen G. Xydis,[7] denotes thirty-three pages to an almost verbatim account of the conference and interviews among the interested parties which took place at that time.

Archbishop Makarios, as the leader of the Greek Cypriot struggle for the union of Cyprus and Greece, at first refused[8] to accept the Agreement reached between Greece and Turkey at Zurich. The chief reason for this opposition to the plan put to him was its entrenched unalterable nature which was to be enshrined in Article 82 of the proposed Constitution of the Republic of Cyprus. However, the situation in Cyprus, was becoming catastrophic and the Archbishop was put under tremendous pressure[9] to sign by the British and Greek delegates to the Conference.

He finally signed when, in addition to the mounting bloodshed in Cyprus, he was informed by the British Colonial Secretary, Mr. Lennox Boyd, that if he persisted in his refusal Britain would carry out a partition of Cyprus between the Greek and Turkish communities. In the absence of Greek support, Archbishop Makarios was forced to sign in order to preserve the unity of Cyprus. The Treaties which were signed were the Draft Treaty of Establishment between U.K., Greece, Turkey and the Republic of Cyprus, the Draft Treaty of Guarantee between U.K., Greece, Turkey and the Republic of Cyprus, the Draft Treaty of Alliance between Greece, Turkey and the Republic of Cyprus, and the Draft Constitution of the Republic of Cyprus.[10]

There is little doubt that Archbishop Markarios signed all the Treaties submitted to him under conditions of duress and moral blackmail.

The Constitution of the Republic of Cyprus, is so detailed that it occupies eighty-three pages of the official text and it lacks juridical validity as understood in terms of modern international law: it is a typical Constitution imposed by force and maintained by the threat of force.

The Treaties introduced legislation that destroyed the hopes of the Greek Cypriots and in particular put an end to the struggle against British Colonialsim waged since 1955. Makarios was unsatisfied with the Treaties as well. Article 1 of the Constitution proclaimed: 'The State of Cyprus is an independent and sovereign Republic with a presidential regime, the President Greek and the Vice-President being Turk elected by the Greek and the Turkish communities of Cyprus respectively as hereinafter in this Constitution provided.'[12] This declaration, however, only masked a state of affairs which can only be described as unique in its political inadequacy. The Treaties excluded both the union of Cyprus with Greece, and partition. They purported to give Cyprus the status of an independent sovereign state, and as such it was accepted both as a member of the United Nations and the British Commonwealth. Yet, the rights which Greece and Turkey were given over the new Republic made a mockery of its independence. First, all the Treaties and Agreements placing the Republic of Cyprus in a subordinate position and shackling its sovereignty were to run in perpetuity. Secondly, the Draft Constitution of the Republic, drafted by the Greek and Turkish Governments, and not by the Cypriots themselves, contained in it provisions for the separation at all levels between the Greek and Turkish communities in Cyprus, making this very same Constitution virtually unworkable. The result was quasi-independence under an impossible and intricate Constitution which was, as events turned out, a perfect instrument for the destruction of the Republic through the separation of the two communities leading to virtual partition, despite the exclusion of partition by the Treaties signed in London. It is obvious from what transpired after the birth of the Republic that the Turkish side, including both the Turkish Cypriots and the various Turkish Governments, never had any serious intention of honourably working the Constitution but only using it to destroy the new State of Cyprus and procure the partition and annexation of Cypriot territory in this way, by the backdoor so to speak.

The Draft Constitution signed by Archbishop Makarios in London in 1959 became the Constitution[13] of the Republic of Cyprus in 1960. The Constitution[14] of the new Republic provided for a Greek Cypriot President and a Turkish Cypriot Vice-President. The President is the Head of the Greek community, and the Vice-President is the Head of the Turkish community. Therefore, the Vice-President is excluded from representing or deputising for the President of the Republic. These functions are held by the President of the House of Representatives who is a Greek (Article 36, p.p. 105-106). In other words, no Turk can represent a Greek and no Greek can represent a Turk. Needless to say, both the Greek President and the Turkish Vice-President of the Republic are elected not by the whole people but by their own separate communities, (Articles 1 and 39). The Constitution having provided for the separation between the President and the Vice-President as Heads of State goes on to provide for a similar separation in executing legislation. Thus, Article 46 of the Constitution ensures that the President and the Vice-President of the Republic should act through a Council of Ministers consisting of ten members, seven of whom are to be appointed by the President of the Republic and three by the Vice-President, i.e. seven Greek and three Turkish Ministers. The Greek and Turkish Ministers are to be nominated and dismissed by the President and the Vice-President respectively, thus ensuring the lack of any cabinet solidarity and responsibility. The Articles of the Constitution dealing with the powers of the President and the Vice-President cite numerous instances where they can act either jointly or independently. However, a most important aspect of the Constitution lies in the power of veto either by the President or the Vice-President. Any decisions made by the Council of Ministers concerning Foreign Affairs, Defence or Security, can be returned to them for reconsideration or vetoed. (Articles: 48, 49, 57.) Moreover, the right of final veto is also extended to any law or decision of the House of Representatives concerning Foreign Affairs, Defence or Security or, again, laws can be returned for reconsideration. (Article: 50 and 51), or referred to the Supreme Constitutional Court. It can be seen from all this that the veto emerges as a Vice-Presidential prerogative, structured to enable the Vice-President, as Head of the Turkish Community, to keep a stranglehold on all executive and legislative functions of the State. Xydis says that, 'the basic structure of the Republic of Cyprus placed a minority—the Turkish Cypriot community—in a privileged position in both government and administration. Because of his veto powers, the Turkish Vice-President was really just another President or a co-President.'[15] The principle of separation between the two communities was also applied to the House of Representatives—that is the Parliament of the Republic. There was going to be no joint electoral roll. 70 per cent of the Members were to be elected by the Greek

Community and 30 percent by the Turkish community.[16]

The legislation of the House of Representatives was limited to 'all matters except those expressly reserved to the Communal Chambers.' (Article 61). Also, under Article 78, voting concerning any modification of the electoral law and the adoption of any law relating to the Municipalities and of any law imposing duties or taxes requires separate majorities of the Greek and Turkish Members voting separately.

The spirit of separation between the two communities was also ensured by the two Communal Chambers, (Article 86), to be set up by the respective communities to have exclusive legislative competence with regard to all religious, educational and cultural matters; personal status; the composition etc. of courts dealing with civil disputes relating to personal status and to religious matters, matters where the interests and institutions are of a purely communal nature; imposition of personal taxes and fees on members of the communities; in matters where subsidiary legislation etc. is required for the setting up of separate Municipalities; in matters relating to the exercise of the authority of control of various producers and consumer co-operatives etc.

Thus the Communal Chambers were designed to be special legislative assemblies of a personal rather than a territorial nature. It is interesting to note that in many countries, where there are some religious and ethnic differences and minorities exist, communal chambers exist on a voluntary basis and are not part of the Constitution of the State. However by including the Communal Chambers[17] in the Constitution of the Republic of Cyprus, it enhanced the separation of the two communites on a purely personal and cultural level, thus making it difficult, if not impossible, *for a Cypriot sentiment to emerge in the new State.*

The same principle of separation was applied to the structure of the Courts. Article 133 dealing with the Supreme Constitutional Court provided a Tribunal composed of a Greek, a Turkish and a neutral Judge. It is interesting to note that owing to a deadlock between the Greek and the Turkish points of view the neutral Judge, who was the President of the Court, never in fact assumed office and the Court never came to function. The inferior Courts, both civil and criminal, were subject to the same principle of division as the political structure of the State. Article 159 provided that in all cases where the parties belonged to the same community they could only be tried by judges belonging to their community. It is obvious from this that the Constitution envisaged separate courts for the two communities, making nonsense of any concept of unity for the Republic and its laws, because it applied to all fields of law not already under the jurisdiction of tribunals dependent on the Communal Chambers. This division was not only entirely unnecessary, but, what was more important, detrimental to the cause of justice. The very concept of Justice defies separation.[18]

Next, the principle of separation is applied in full force to the Public Services and the Security Forces. The Constitution provides that 70 percent of the public servants and members of the police forces were to be Greek Cypriots and 30 percent Turkish Cypriots. This 7:3 ratio was not, however, to be applied to the armed forces of the Republic. There the ratio was meant to be 6:4 and a complicated system of appointment was worked out whereby each commander was to have a deputy belonging to a different community and appointed by the head of that community, i.e. the President and the Vice-President. Bearing in mind that the actual composition of the population of Cyprus at that time was roughly 82 percent Greek and 18 percent Turkish and that the chiefs of the armed forces were to derive their authority from different sources (the President and the Vice-President) it is no wonder that no armed forces of the Republic of Cyprus came into being before the crisis of December 1963.

Then, under Article 173, the Constitution provided for the establishment of separate Turkish municipalities at Nicosia, Limassol, Larnaca and Paphos. Obviously here the principle of separation between the two communities found its basic territorial expression, and it was the opposition of President Makarios to this virtual territorial partition of the Republic which provided the Turkish community, inspired as always from Ankara, with the pretext to stage their breakaway from the Republic of Cyprus in December 1963.

All this proves that the Zurich and London agreements were an obvious defeat for Greek foreign policy.[19] 'All maintained that under this Cyprus settlement the new State of Cyprus would be neither independent nor free. Most of the critics termed the island's proposed new status a condominium, a triple condominium: a few called it a protectorate. And some maintained that Cyprus was being placed under a triple occupation. The new state, they observed, would be based on alliances concluded even before the state had been born. These alliances deprived the Cypriots of any possibility to exercise their right of self-determination and to conduct an independent foreign policy. They imposed upon Cyprus commitments or servitudes—for instance, through the presence of foreign troops on the island's territory under the Treaty of Alliance, or through the right of intervention under the Treaty of Guarantee. And they would be susceptible to no revision, since they were to be considered as fundamental and non-amendable articles of the Constitution.'[20]

The Turks derived every advantage from the fact that they were a minority in Cyprus, and in order to redress the balance exercised every pressure to influence the text of the Treaties and Agreements which, upon closer reading, are fairly advantageous to Turkey.

The Constitution itself was a political mockery. No Cypriot elements, whether Greek or Turkish, had anything to do with the framing of their Constitution. This makes the 1960 Constitution of the Republic of Cyprus a typical colonial constitution imposed by a ruling power on a dependent territory, and it is no different if not worse, from the British Constitution,[21] imposed upon Cyprus until 1931.

It is quite evident that the President of the Republic was envisaged by the Constitution to be merely the head of the Greek community and the Vice-President the head of the Turkish community, whose main functions were not the smooth functioning of the Government but the representation and protection of their two distinct communities. The Constitution provided for co-operation between the two chief executives, but no machinery for solving any deadlock reached between them by the use of the veto. The Council of Ministers was not responsible to one head but the Greek Members were responsible to the Greek President and the Turkish Members to the Turkish Vice-President and formed in fact their own respective cabinets. Therefore, a meeting of the Council of Ministers of the Republic was really a joint session of two separate and, in reality, rival Governments, yet exercising authority over the same territory which was a contradiction to be exploited by the Turkish minority to the full. The Legislators (the House of Representatives), being elected on separate electoral rolls, were a joint session of two separate parliaments representing two separate peoples and voting separately on all important issues.

The basic principle of the 1960 Constitution, therefore, was the setting up of a 'Vice-Presidential Regime' because of the excessive powers of the Turkish Vice-President and of the obstructive nature of his privileges. The veto possessed by the Turkish Vice-President acting as the head of a minority, created a unique constitutional situation making the functioning of the Government impossible. The Government of the Republic of Cyprus became a 'diarchy' but a hostile diarchy, and this made the Constitution a sure recipe for failure.

Without examining in detail the attempts to apply the Constitution of 1960 up to December 1963, it would be well to interpret the general consequences of the regime established in 1960. The Turkish slogan of 'Cyprus is Turkish' became somewhat of a reality. Turkey was the protector under the Treaties of a minority in Cyprus, and this gave her the advantage over Greece and Britain. Her presence and influence were constanly required to redress the balance between the two communities. The Constitution forced on Cyprus by Turkey was explained by the necessity to protect the Turkish minority from discrimination, but, in fact, by loading the Turkish minority with privileges, it established virtual domination of the Cypriot Government by exercising its veto. Any attempt by the Greek Cypriot majority to emancipate itself from this Turkish yoke would then be interpreted as an attempt to intimidate and discriminate against the Turkish minority and would give Turkey the opportunity to act under the Treaties to annex either the whole or a part of Cyprus. This has been the aim of both the Turkish leadership in Cyprus and the various Governments in Ankara. They saw the Constitution of 1960 not as a means to further the cause of a truly independent Cyprus but to destroy it. It was only various events which postponed this eventuality over a period of years.

The part played by Greece throughout this period is not very clear. The union of Cyprus with Greece has never been the first choice of the Greek political leaders or the majority of the Greek people. Greece never really backed the Cypriot campaign for enosis and, in 1959 in Zurich, and later in London, the then Greek Government failed to support Archbishop Makarios. It is, interesting to note what Constantine Karamanlis, Greek Premier, said to Archbishop Markarios when the latter refused to sign the agreements in London, 'I draw you attention to the consequences of your attitude and must declare the following: I neither desire nor am able to press you to take part in the conference and sign the agreements. I inform you, however, that I shall protect the honour of Greece, which accepted the invitation to the conference after your assent and I shall go to the conference. I also declare that by signing these agreements, my Government ends its Cypriot policy. You are free, if you wish, to continue the struggle alone.'[23]

The policy of subsequent Greek governments had to follow a similar pattern and yield to Turkish action throughout all the shades of the Cyprus crisis from 1963 to the Turkish invasion of 1974. This must be seen as the obvious consequence of the fact that Cyprus has always been remote as far as Greece is concerned. The Greeks of Cyprus are as remote from Athens as were the Greeks of Alexandria, and the gap of centuries of separation cannot be bridged by the enthusiasm of a few decades. Greece since the end of the Second World War has been the victim of major political and economic upheavals. Throughout the whole of this period the main threat to established Greek society comes from the political left. In other words, the problems which preoccupied Greek politics were those of defence both internal and external against the communist states to the north of Greece. For this reason, Greece joined N.A.T.O. in 1951 and all Greek Governments have always followed a subservient policy in respect of the principal N.A.T.O. powers, i.e. U.S.A. and Britain, in order to survive politically, militarily and financially. Such a position of weakness placed Greece in the position of a vassal state (vassalage is nowadays politely called inter-dependence.) As a vassal of U.S.A. and Britain, Greece could not, and did not, feel inclined to challenge American and British support of Turkey—the cornerstone of Western defence in the Eastern Mediterranean. This is how it came about that Greece abandoned Cyprus and allowed Turkey, by means of the Turkish minority in Cyprus, to deprive the Republic of Cyprus of sovereignty, authority, and, finally, territory. Unless there is a fundamental change of heart in Greece in respect of the cause of Cyprus, the Turkish invasion and partial occupation of Cyprus is going to be the first stage of the reannexation of the whole of the island by Turkey, leading to the restoration of the status of 1878. In a way, the Turkish invasion of Cyprus in 1974 marks the ultimate end of the British period in Cyprus. Once more, as in 1878, the Turkish Crescent has been hoisted over Nicosia. How long it is going to stay there is now something which the Great Powers will ultimately have to settle as executors of the will and spirit of the United Nations, or, failing that, the responsibility falls on Greece and the policy of its leaders.

II
The Years of Adjustment

Archbishop Makarios, on his return to Cyprus on 1st March 1959, was given an enthusiastic welcome by the Greek Cypriots. He declared: 'we have triumphed, today Cyprus is free.' As things have eventually proved, there was no triumph and in fact Cyprus was less free to determine its destiny than ever before. Few Greek Cypriots could honestly consider the new state of affairs as a triumph for their cause, and Makarios himself, much more than anybody else, did not believe in his own brave words.[1] According to seasoned observers, there was little enthusiasm in Cyprus for the new 'free' Republic. Those Greeks of Cyprus who had fought and suffered, had done so for something different. The first important consequence of the new state of affairs was the fractioning of the Greek Cypriot front. Differences of opinion between Archbishop Makarios, as the political supremo of the Greek Cypriots, and George Grivas, the leader of the armed struggle, now came to the fore. The Greek Cypriots certainly did not get what they had bargained for. They did not yet fully realize their predicament, but many instinctively came to question the leadership of Archbishop Makarios by supporting a party which put forward a rival candidate for the presidential elections. This party, the Democratic Union, led by John Clerides, stood to the right of Makarios by dedicating itself to the ideal of enosis and were immediately supported in this by the pro-communist party, A.K.E.L.[2] The presidential electoral campaign only existed for the Greeks as they had two candidates.[3] Among the Turkish community there was no election at all. Their single candidate Dr. F. Kuchuk was simply proclaimed Vice-President by the Turkish community. The same phenomenon occurred during

Makarios, amongst the ruins of the Presidential Palace.

Makarios returns to Cyprus, 7th December 1974.

Archbishop Makarios visits refugee camp.

the election to the House of Representatives (the Parliament of Cyprus). The thirty-five Greek Cypriot Members were split across a spectrum ranging from the extreme right to the extreme left, whereas the fifteen Turkish Cypriot Members all belonged to Dr. Kuchuk's party. Thus, the Turkish minority in the new Republic was not only privileged but also united, whereas the Greek majority became neutralized through its own fractioning, caused by the basic political failure of the Greek Cypriots at that time, and a result of a pro-Turkish situation arising out of the Zurich-London agreements.

Undoubtedly, at this point, Archbishop Makarios, now President of the Republic, had to realize that the struggle he had waged against British colonialism could not result in the union of Cyprus with Greece, but it was nevertheless a step towards that end in the future. Logically speaking, it would be hardly difficult for a truly independent Cyprus to exercise its rights of self-determination and join itself to Greece. The main endeavour now towards this end was to establish and defend the independence of the new State. Precisely because of this, the leadership of the Turkish minority and the Ankara Government could have no interest in a truly independent Cyprus. Turkey, from the beginning, decided to use the Constitution to paralyze the working of the State in order to produce a crisis that would destroy it, thus entailing Turkish intervention under the Treaties of Guarantee resulting at least in some form of partition of the island.[4] There is no doubt that Turkish preparations for the destruction and ultimate partition of Cyprus were now in an advanced stage, as the examination of some outstanding events from 1960-63 will show.

The political life of the Republic of Cyprus in 1960 began on a sour note. Archbishop Markarios had gone on record to declare that he had signed the Zurich-London agreements under pressure, and that the national aim (enosis) remained unchanged. Because of this the Turkish Representatives of the House refused to congratulate him on his assession to the Presidency. The politics of Cyprus were now destined to a struggle for control, with the Greek Cypriots hoping to amend the Constituion to make it more workable and the Turks striving for increased separation between the two communities.

In other words, the post-independence period was a 'peaceful' continuation of the struggle between Greeks and Turks. This struggle was conducted on several different levels simultaneously, which underlined the fact that the Constitution was a battleground for new inter-communal strife.

The first area of strife arose with the civil service. After 1878 the British rulers of Cyprus continued the Ottoman adminstration of the island, which was mostly staffed by Turks and Armenians. Gradually, however, particularly after Cyprus had become a British Crown Colony, in 1925, the Greeks of Cyprus, being the majority of the population, came to supply the bulk of the personnel of the administrative services. Due to education progress during the British period, the Greek community pulled rapidly ahead of the Turkish in the proportion of school and university graduates. This was also paralleled in the economic sector. Thus, by the 1950s, the number of Greeks and Turks in the civil service of British Cyprus came to be roughly proportional to the population ratios, and, in many Departments the Greek ratio was higher than that of the population. The Constitution of 1960, however, laid down in Article 123, that the two communities must be represented at all levels of the public service in a 7:3 ratio.[5] The Turkish Cypriots began pressing for immediate application of the ratio and immediately asserted that they were being passed over in favour of the Greeks, while the Greeks asserted that there were not enough qualified Turkish candidates and that the quota system 'put a premium on a candidate's race rather than his abilities'.[6] The Turks particulary alleged that many posts were filled over the heads of qualified Turks by unqualified Greeks as long as they were ex-E.O.K.A. men. The battle over the civil service appointments is illustrated by the fact that by 1963 no fewer than 2,000 civil service appointments had been contested on communal grounds before the Constitutional Court. If the Turks had succeeded in having all these appointments declared as invalid, this 'would have meant the collapse of the whole administration'[7], which was, perhaps, the aim of the Turkish tactics.

The next major struggle in the new Republic concerned

taxation. Taxation had always been a major weapon in the Near East for coercing and crippling minorities, and the Turkish Government was a past-master of such tactics. The Constitution of 1960 ensured that each community in Cyprus would tax itself by means of the Communal Chambers, and that any taxation relating to both communities had to be passed by separate majorities in the House of Representatives, thus giving the Turkish minority the power of veto. (Article 78 of Constitution). By March 1961, it became evident that the House of Representatives was unable to pass any legislation concerning taxation. This meant that the Executive could not collect taxes. President Makarios was forced to order all officials to collect taxes as usual and this action was denounced by Mr. R. Denktash as 'unconstitutional and illegal' and he urged all Turkish importers 'to refuse to pay duties or taxes illegally demanded.'[8] In December 1961, the Turkish Representatives voted against a new income tax bill, in spite of the fact that the bill had previously been passed by the Council of Ministers, including the Turkish Ministers and Dr. Kuchuk the Vice-President. The chief Turkish objections to financial legislation were that they wanted it to be reviewed annually if possible, so that they could exercise their power of veto over the finances of the Republic each year. Meanwhile, Greeks and Turks continued to pay a form of income tax to their respective Communal Chambers. There was never any tax legislation passed under the Constitution up to 1963.[9] In February, 1963, the Supreme Constitutional Court ruled that the Government had no right to collect customs dues or income tax because of the lack of the Turkish separate vote in the House of Representatives. The Government 'ignored'[10] this decision. At no point during this dispute did the Turkish leadership assert that the proposed legislature was discriminatory against the Turkish minority. The Turkish refusal was merely the part of a larger battle to break down the efficacy of the State in a wider struggle over the Constitution.[11] The payment of taxes to the Communal Chambers created a fiscal partition of the island between the two communities. There is no doubt that the Turkish community suffered because of this, for being much poorer it had to provide for a population scattered throughout the island.

From the above can be sensed an enormous Turkish reluctance to pay taxes to what they considered was a principally Greek State. The creation of the Communal Chambers made such a stand possible. The only way in which the State could have collected taxes from the Turkish community would have been to accede to the demand of the Turkish leaders for an annual stranglehold over the finances of the Republic, which they wanted to exercise not in order to protect their community from discriminatory taxation but to force further concessions from the State on the road to partition. On the other hand, in the circumstances, President Makarios and his advisers had perhaps no immediate understanding of the Turkish poverty in Cyprus, and a more generous use of development funds on behalf of the Turkish community might have shifted their allegiance somewhat in the direction of peaceful co-existence with the Greek majority in the new Republic.

The next clash between the two communities, which brought the purpose of the new State to nullity, was the failure to create the armed forces of the State. Article 129 of the Constitution stated: 'The Republic shall have an army of 2,000 men of whom 60% shall be Greeks and 40% shall be Turks.' This was disproportionate to the population ratio. Yet the Article in question did not provide any further details as to the organization of this force. President Makarios wanted an integrated army whereas the Turks demanded the establishment of separate units down to platoon level: in other words, the creation of a separate Turkish force under the flag of the Republic. It was in respect of the integrated army issue that Dr. Kuchuk was able to exercise for the first and last time his Vice-Presidential veto (20th October 1961). As a consequence of this, President Makarios decided that Cyprus had no need of any armed forces. In the absence of an army loyal to the flag of the Republic, the political leadership of each community tended to become more and more the prisoner of the extremists arming secretly undergound. The green light was given to both sides to create their own forces and armed conflict was made inevitable in the circumstances, awaiting only the required spark to set it off. The spark which finally started the armed conflict in Cyprus in December 1963, was created by the issue of the five separate municipalities. Article 173 of the 1960 Constitution says that separate Turkish municipalities are to be established in the five largest towns of Cyprus, Nicosia, Limassol, Famagusta, Larnaca and Paphos. The same Article, however, goes on to say that the President and the Vice-President shall, within four years of this being in operation, examine the question of whether or not these municipalities should continue to be separate.

Ever since the settlement of the Turks in Cyprus in the 16th Century, they have occupied certain quarters of the island's towns. These quarters, such as the old town of Nicosia and Famagusta, were formally the quarters inhabited by the Latin and Venetian masters of Cyprus. The Turks merely took over their quarters, turning the beautiful Latin Gothic cathedrals into their mosques. These Turkish quarters of the towns were generally separate from the more modern Greek quarters. During the troubles of 1958, the British colonial administration raised these Turkish quarters to the status of separate municipalities, partly to separate the two communities and partly to legitimize the claims of the Turkish minority to a separate existence. As such, they were a part of the attempt to implement the Macmillan Plan of 1958 and, according to the then Greek Foreign Minister, Mr. E. Areroff, the Greek Cypriots themselves at that time wanted the separation of the municipalities for a variety of reasons including important economic factors.[13]

However, in view of the undisguised Turkish desire for partition and the nature of the 1960 Constitution with its stress on separation, the generous ideas of 1958, when enosis seemed round the corner, gave way to fear that separate Turkish municipalities would be a dangerous step towards partition. On the Turkish side, though they became the main issue of how far the Greeks genuinely accepted them as a separate community. Yet, after independence, no legal steps were taken to fix the municipal boundaries. At the end of 1962, President Makarios announced that the Law of 1958 concerning the separate Turkish municipalities, which up to then had been renewed annually, would not be extended. A meeting on Christmas Eve 1962, between the two sides almost achieved agreement for the creation of united municipalities for the period of one year with Turkish and Greek members of the Council being elected on separate rolls and the budget allocated in proportion to the Greek and Turkish population of each municipality. The agreement was drafted jointly by Glafcos Clerides for the Greek Cypriots and R. Denktash for the Turkish Cypriots, but the next day the agreement was rejected by the Turkish Vice-President, Dr. F. Kuchuk, possibly on instructions from Ankara. The Turks claimed that justice was not done to their position of agreeing to re-examine the whole question, but they never agreed in advance to the principle of united municipalities.[14]

In January 1963, the Council of Ministers set up Development Boards to run the towns. The Greek municipalities accepted the Development Boards, but the Turkish ones refused to. The whole question was referred to the Supreme Constitutional Court which ruled that both the Development Boards and the Turkish separate municipalities were invalid. As the Court had already decided a few weeks previously (8th February 1963) that the Turkish veto on the tax laws of 1961 meant that the Government had no authority to collect customs and income tax, both central and local Government were now deprived of their legal ability to function. This complete breakdown was sealed by the resignation of the German Professor, the President of the Supreme Constitutional Court, Dr. Ernst Forsthoff, on Monday 21st May 1963.

The Turkish insistence on separate municipalities was an obvious indication that they were determined to force through separation by all means, and that the creation of separate Turkish municipalities, by giving communal separation a physical entity, was to be the first step towards a full territorial partition, using the powers of the Turkish Communal Chambers to create self-governing Turkish enclaves. Xydis points out:

'Besides, it was not even in the interest of the Turkish Cypriots to set up territorially separate municipalities for these cities, since statistics revealed that they contributed far less than did the Greek Cypriots to the upkeep of these cities. But, in addition to certain economic, legal and technical drawbacks to the establishment of separate municipalities with territorial jurisdiction, political considerations had to be reckoned with, for it was almost mathematically certain that public opinion both in Cyprus and Greece would experience bitter disappointment, if such a right were conceded to the Cypriot Turks. Extremely undesirable repercussions could follow.'[15] Much of the Government was already paralyzed or drifting into illegality in respect of its own Constitution and the Zurich-London agreements. The faults of the 1960 Constitution were now obvious as it could not provide the means for a concerted effort at achieving any unity or understanding between the two communities and became itself the fertile source of constant strife.

'Thus by early 1963 progress towards an efficient civil service and army had foundered. Cyprus was without a customs law, an income tax law or a settlement of the 'battle of the five towns'. The Government had nearly come to a standstill. The stagnating ecomony was dependent on British aid and the income generated by the two British bases. The two communities, increasingly at each other's throats, were hopelessly headed pell-mell for a violent confrontation. Indeed, during the Summer of 1963, incidents of violence and terrorism mounted.'[16]

In view of this, President Makarios took the decisive step of asking the Turkish leadership to consider a review of the Constitution in order to make it more workable. On November 30th 1963, Makarios submitted[17] the following thirteen points for the consideration of his Turkish Vice-President. Copies of the proposals were also submitted to the British, Greek and Turkish Governments for their information:

1. The right of veto of the President and the Vice-President of the Republic to be abandoned.

2. The Vice-President of the Republic to deputise for the President of the Republic in case of his temporary absence or incapacity to perform his duties.

3. The Greek President of the House of Representatives and the Turkish Vice-President to be elected by the

House as a whole and not as under the Constitution, the President by the Greek Members of the House and the Vice-President by the Turkish Members of the House.

4. The Vice-President of the House of Representatives to deputise for the President of the House in case of his temporary absence or incapacity to perform his duties.

5. The constitutional provisions regarding separate majorities for enactment of certain laws by the House of Representatives to be abolished.

6. Unified Municipalities to be established.

7. The administration of Justice to be unified.

8. The division of the Security Forces into Police and Gendarmerie to be abolished.

9. The numerical strength of the Security Forces and of the Defence Forces to be determined by a Law.

10. The proportion of the participation of Greek and Turkish Cypriots in the composition of the Public Service and the Forces of the Republic to be modified in proportion to the ratio of the population of Greek and Turkish Cypriots.

11. The number of the Members of the Public Service Commission to be reduced from ten to five.

12. All decisions of the Public Service Commission to be taken by simple majority.

13. The Constitution provides that there shall be two Communal Chambers, one Greek and one Turkish, each having jurisdiction in matters of religion, education, cultural affairs and personal status over members of its respective community as well as control over communal co-operative societies.

The effect of the Archbishop's thirteen points would have been to abolish some of the provisions for separate communal institutions and rights and to create an integrated united state with some limited guarantees for the Turkish community. It is to be noted that such an arrangement would put an end to the Turkish hope of partition. The thirteen points would have amended the bi-communal character of the Republic of Cyprus and would have made the Cypriot Turks what they have always been, i.e. a minority, although they would have still been a privileged one. Perhaps it was a mistake to put forward all the points simultaneously, because, in the existing climate of mistrust, it enabled the Turks to claim that they were being threatened with extinction and prompted them to go ahead with their preparation for territorial separation. On December 16th, 1963, the Turkish Government without any reference to Dr. Kuchuk and his advisers, rejected the proposals of President Makarios.[18] This rejection increased the tension between the two communities, reviving the situation of 1958 despite all appeals by Archbishop Makarios and Dr. Kuchuk for calm. Within five days of the Turkish rejection 'shooting'[19] began between Greeks and Turks, starting in Nicosia and then spreading to the rest of Cyprus as both Greek and Turkish armed organizations emerged from underground. The incidents of the 21st and 22nd December, 1963, marked the beginning of the fighting between the two communities, which lasted until the Spring of 1964, and brought to an end the structure of the Republic of Cyprus of 1960. As the fighting got underway, the Turkish leader gained the Turkish community from the Republic of Cyprus because by seizing certain areas the Turks had carried out a de facto partition by establishing Turkish territorial areas in many localities of the Republic. The first Turkish area to be organised was the Turkish quarter of Nicosia which became marked off from the rest of the town by the so-called 'Green Line'.[20]

The whole history of modern Cyprus since it began to emerge from British colonial rule until the moment of writing has been marked by a bitter conflict between the Greek and Turkish communities inhabiting the island, causing the dissolution of the ill-started Republic. The whole issue has been swathed in wads of hypocrisy. Practically every official publication emanating from the Greek Government of Cyprus goes out of its way to portray the Greek majority as being deeply in love with the Turkish minority—love which is, unfortunately, unrequited. An example of paying no attention to the realities of the situation is the publication of photographs from Cyprus showing mosques in close proximity to Christian Churches with such captions attached as 'Christian

Church and Mosque, for Centuries they have existed in peace.' The idea of brotherly love is clearly expressed. The facts, however, speak differently. The very fact that a Moslem Mosque has been erected near a Christian Church shows it to be a monument (as indeed it is) to a brutal Moslem conquest of a Christian country and community.

Mosques erected in the middle of ancient Christian towns are monuments to the passage of conquerors. Are such scenes a proof that the conquered love their masters or that previous masters loved their subjects? It has been pointed out that the Turks in Cyprus mistrust and fear the Greeks because the Greeks, with the independence of Cyprus, gave the impression of trying to humiliate and exclude them. The original intention of the Greek Cypriots was union with Greece. The desire for union with Greece was whole-heartedly felt by the whole Greek population of Cyprus. If, according to the doctrine of national self-determination a plebiscite had been held in Cyprus, it would have resulted in the union of the island with Greece. The Turkish minority, instigated by Britain and aided by Turkey, prevented the Greeks from exercising their right of self-determination thus preventing unity with Greece. For doing this they hardly earned the love of their fellow Greek islanders, nor did they deserve to do so. Furthermore, in an independent Cyprus, as adequately illustrated above, the Turkish minority strained every nerve to destroy the Republic of Cyprus and to partition its territory. No wonder then, when fighting broke out, that the Greeks had prepared an armed organization to wage the struggle, and it is hardly surprising that there were more Turkish casualties, if only because the Turks were outnumbered in most cases. Reference has been made by many authors to the atrocities carried out by the Greeks against the Turkish population in the fighting of 1963-64, but those commenting on this state of affairs seem to adopt an *a priori* attitude that the Greeks should have loved the Turks. To have expected the Greek Cypriots to behave otherwise, one expresses a relative ignorance of human nature.

Future historians might find that Archbishop Makarios in his Christian principles and his desire to implement them, tried to live up to this image of love thy neighbour as theyself as applied to his Turkish minority. If so, he has been, no doubt, martyred for them.

III
Intercommunal Friction

There is clear evidence that, after years of armed struggle, both communities did not expect any peaceful solution to their problem. Many arms held by E.O.K.A. and the Turkish T.M.T.[1] organization remained with the hardcore of these organizations after 1960. Even before independence arms were being smuggled[2] in for the Turkish Cypriots from Turkey. Early in 1962, ex-members of VOLKAN, the Turkish Resistance Organization, revived the T.M.T., and soon there were 2,500 armed and partially trained men on the Turkish side, receiving help from the Turkish military contingent stationed in Cyprus under the Treaties. On the Greek side, ex-E.O.K.A. men were forming themselves into irregular units getting their arms from Government stocks held for the purposes of the eventual creation of the armed forces and from the Greek contingent stationed on the island. Both sides were obviously expecting, sooner or later, an armed settlement.[3] Once shooting began on the 21st December 1963, there were enough armed men on both sides to spread the conflict throughout the island. It was evident that if the Greek Cypriots tried to alter the Constitution the Turkish community would try to seize large areas of Cyprus in order to carry out a partition and, perhaps, bring about Turkish intervention. Therefore, in the event of fighting breaking out the Greeks had to move fast in order to prevent such a situation. As events turned out, they did not move fast enough.

After the events of the 21st December 1963, fighting escalated every day until a major battle was fought in Nicosia on Christmas Eve, spreading to other parts of Cyprus on Christmas Day.[4] Fitful negotiations took place between

Archbishop Makarios and Dr. F. Kuchuk who met for the last time on 24th December 1963. From that day onwards, there was to be no further personal contact between the two leaders. Meanwhile, Turkey was threatening to invade Cyprus, the British Secretary for Commonwealth Relations, Duncan Sandys, flew to Cyprus on 28th December 1963, and the Turkish army contingent seized the most strategic position on the island across the Nicosia-Kyrenia road. At this low ebb in Turkish fortunes, the 650-man Turkish army contingent established in Cyprus under the Treaty of Alliance, took decisive (and almost certainly pre-planned) action. Without referring to the tripartite H.Q. as it should have done under the treaty, it marched out of its camp north of Nicosia on the 25th, and took up positions at Orta Kerry (Minzelli) and Geuneli on either side of the Nicosia-Kyrenia road, the historic jugular vein of the island.[5]

Makarios had agreed 'on the 26th December 1963, that British troops from the Sovereign British Bases should form a buffer zone between the two communities in Nicosia, thus on the 26th December, under command of Major-General Peter Young, Army Commander in the Sovereign British Base Areas, the first British troops moved into the Republic to begin their brief but immensely difficult task of keeping the peace . . .'[6]

The setting up of various buffer zones between the two communities was the beginning of permanent Turkish enclaves in Cyprus, which became dependent on Turkey and thus partitioned the island *de facto*[7] between the two communities although this fact remained disguised for a long time by diplomatic verbiage.

In mid-February 1964, a general battle developed in Limassol which looked like provoking a Turkish invasion and prompted Britain to appeal to the Security Council. On the 4th March 1964, on the day of the Security Council Resolution to establish a Peace-Keeping[8] force for Cyprus for three months, another major battle took place at Ktima which caused much bloodshed. On March 24th, a Finnish diplomat and former Premier, Sakari Tuomioja, was appointed by the U.N. Secretary General, U Thant, as mediator for Cyprus. The first U.N. units (UNFICYP) arrived on the 27th March and took up their official peace-keeping duties on the island.

The arrival of UNFICYP did not halt the shipment of arms to Cyprus for both sides. On the Greek side, now that the Turks had succeeded, a national guard[9] was formed and on the 4th April a determined attack was made on the north-western coastal villages of Kokkina and Mansoura where the Turks had established a bridge-head for import of arms and the landing[10] of irregulars from Turkey.

In the meantime, the most significant consequence of the battle between the Greeks and Turks was the return to the island of General Grivas in the Summer of 1964, with his firm ideas about enosis and discipline. The leadership of Makarios became overshadowed from that moment onwards, as Grivas took over the command of the National Guard. In August 1964, another major skirmish took place in the Kokkina-Mansoura area which entailed the intervention of the Turkish airforce. Fighting broke out on 3rd August and continued on the 5th and 6th 'during which time Turkish airforce fighters invaded Cyprus air space and attacked Government positions overlooking the enclave as well as traffic moving along the roads in the vicinity.'[11] The Cyprus Government, under the pressure of Turkish threats about an imminent invasion of the island brought the matter before the United Nations. The result was another of those unfortunate stalemates so characteristic of the post-1945 World. Makarios failed to get the hoped for support from Greece and Russia, and the Security Council managed to persuade Turkey that the Turkish air attacks conflicted with Article 2:3 of the U.N. Charter; Turkey ceased her air attacks; Greece and Russia were let off the hook; and every Turkish enclave in Cyprus now became a true part of Cyprus protected[12] by the forces of UNFICYP. The Turks could now take stock of their advantages. There were Turkish enclaves in all the major towns except Kyrenia. In the Lefka area there were some 8,000 Turks, including nearly 1,000 members of the T.M.T., in a good position to join up with any landing near Xeros. The big enclave north of Nicosia almost reached the sea at Temblos in the Kyrenia district. At Ktima the Turkish position overlooked the coast from an excellent defensive position. The Larnaca enclave commanded a piece of coast ideal for the use of light landing-craft. At Kophinou, the strong Turkish position controlled the main roads from Nicosia to Limassol and Larnaca; in addition to this, every Turkish village in Cyprus was an armed nest. According to the *Economist*, in November 1964, the British troops were very much on the side of the Turks: 'That their sympathies lie with the Turks is undeniable; it has become inherent in the situation... Unhappily, a fair percentage of British officers and N.C.O.'s fought against E.O.K.A. in the 1955-1959 troubles and they seem to have long memories.'[13] Moreover, according to Stegenga, 'by establishing Green Line neutral zones to separate the two communities in Nicosia, Larnaca and elsewhere, the British were tacitly partitioning parts of the country.'[14]

The next major armed clash between the two communities took place again on 15th November 1967, at Agios Theodoros. The importance of this clash lay in that it brought about a renewed confrontation between Greece and Turkey and was terminated by the removal of General Grivas to Greece. During this fight, which spread to the neighbouring village of Kophinou, 24 Turks were killed, and one Greek. A reasonably effective ceasefire was quickly brought into effect. Greece, besides withdrawing Grivas, was forced by Turkey to withdraw their 10-12,000 Greek National Soldiers, who were illegally on Cyprus. The new Athens dictatorial regime complied.

By this time, the island had become effectively, although not actually, partitioned. The Turks had had their way as they now commanded a territorial base economically dependent on Turkey. It is interesting here to show the contrast between the Greek and Turkish positions in Cyprus. Both countries maintained contingents on the island, but Turkey had the marked advantage over Greece that she controlled the Turkish enclaves: on the Greek Cypriot side Cyprus was both economically and politically unconnected with Greece. In view of subsequent events this virtual annexation of parts of the island's territory by Turkey had been overlooked by nearly all the commentators upon the Cypriot scene. The formation all over Cyprus of the autonomous Turkish areas was the direct result of the intervention of British troops both before and after they were placed under the UNFICYP. This British effort to solve a problem which they themselves had created was well understood by the Government of Archbishop Makarios.[15]

When the period 1964-1974 is looked at in retrospect, it can be seen that the Turkish success removed the communal aspect of the Constitution of the Republic of Cyprus. The government of President Makarios rejected[16] the Zurich-London agreements. However, the rejection of the agreements could do nothing to remove the Greek and Turkish contingents from the island, which were there under these agreements. In reality, the Government of President Makarios was now faced with three military occupations, i.e. Greek, Turkish and U.N., each of the parties had a vested interest in the survival of the Makarios Government as a means toward the re-establishment of the pre-1963 status. The Government of President Makarios, taking stock of the situation, could claim that although they had lost some territory to the Turks, they had got rid of the Treaties and the Constitution had lost its unworkable bi-communal character. A purely Greek Cypriot Government could function quite smoothly within the framework of the 1960 Constitution. The safest path, as it turned out to be, was for this Government to become committed to the cause of independence and non-alignment.[17]

Within the framework of a now independent Cyprus, diplomatic activity originating in the U.N. got busy to provide an opportunity for an understanding between the two communities. With a stubborn determination to disregard the basic fact that the Greek and Turkish elements could not function in Cyprus on an equal footing as envisaged by the 1960 Constitution, the Secretary-General of U.N. appointed a number of Mediators between the two communities, in order to promote N.A.T.O. harmony in the Eastern Mediterranean. The first, Mr. S. Tuomioja, of Finland, who died soon afterwards in 1964, was accepted by Ankara[18] because to the racialism of Turkish mentality his ancestry linked him remotely with the Turks. The next Mediator was Senor Galo Plaza, ex-President of Ecuador. This new Mediator, with his Latin American background, could be said to have been completely out of place in the typically near-eastern setting of Cyprus. Somehow, it seems that he saw the Greek and Turkish Cypriots as being similar to the Hispanised and non-Hispanised Indian communities of some Latin-American countries. In such countries the efficacy of the regimes had come to be measured by the success in bringing the Indian population within the urban-European Spanish culture. How can one otherwise explain the opening passage of Galo Plaza's Report which declares: 'Little was done under any of the previous regimes . . . to bridge the separation of the Greek Cypriot and Turkish Cypriot communities.'[19] This statement ignores the historical fact that the previous regimes had been Turkish and British, and the latter had no interest either in creating a unified community in Cyprus or imposing British culture on the island. Above all, the British as leaseholders had no right to impose the Greek culture of the majority on the Turkish minority. Galo Plaza tried to blame the colonial administration for difficulties it did not create and which it could do very little to reconcile, even if it had tried to impose its own culture.

After this, Galo Plaza did come to the conclusion that the Turkish Cypriots were a minority, and that they had been endowed by the Zurich-London Agreements and the Constitution with over-generous privileges. He then went on to observe that the Turks had modified their insistence on partition to 'physical separation under a Federal Government.'[20] Though the latter can hardly be distinguished from partition under the particular circumstances of Cyprus, as Galo Plaza observed himself by his words that such an arrangement would 'inevitably lead to partition.' Galo Plaza's main objections to the partition of Cyprus were economic and social, providing a constant source of friction between the two hostile populations. This is a sound argument except that separation between the Greeks and Turks could not be socially disruptive, as the two communities never formed one integral community anyway. His chief objection, however, to partition was caused by the concept of the forcible resettlement of the population which he declared to be 'contrary to all the enlightened principles of the present time, including those set forth in the Universal Declaration of Human Rights,' and he goes on to describe it as 'a desparate step in the wrong direction.'[21]

However, the hardship and misery caused by the mixing on an equal basis of incompatible peoples is much greater than that which can be caused by their separation. It is to be noted that in the event the Turkish plan for partition did not envisage a full scale separation of the two peoples but rather a gradual transfer phased over a great number of years. Yet Gala Plaza even disliked this gradual uprooting. The Mediator's rejection of any separation in Cyprus came to influence his suggestions for the solution of the problem. He went on record to say that the Turks of Cyprus had no reason to fear Greek rule and that there was a definite possibility of the two communities living together in peace. His suggestion was that the Cypriot Turks should enjoy special safeguards and he mentions in the Constitution of Cyprus the 'human rights and fundamental freedoms conforming with those set forth in the Universal Declaration of Human Rights adopted by the United Nations and judicial procedures for their application; and vigilance to ensure equal treatment in appointments and promotions in the public services.' Furthermore, the Turkish minority was to have 'a continuation of the previous autonomy in certain fields, of religion, education and personal status.' Together with 'representation . . . in the governmental institutions.' He had obviously failed to read in the 1960 Constitution of Cyprus, a whole section entitled 'Fundamental Rights and Liberties', modelled on those set forth in the 'European Convention for the Protection of Human Rights and Fundamental Freedoms and the U.N. Universal Declaration of Human Rights.' The final proposal of Galo Plaza was that the 'problem of Cyprus cannot be resolved by attempting to restore the situation which existed before December 1963.'[22]

Yet the solution proposed was precisely a return to square one, with the difference that the Turks would now have fewer rights and guarantees than before. This was due to the fact that Galo Plaza insisted on the repealing of the Treaties of 1960 in order to make Cyprus fully sovereign. The guarantees for the Turks proposed by the Galo Plaza Report were that the U.N. should act as a guarantor, receiving immediately any complaint about any possible violation, and that a U.N. Commissioner should be appointed 'whose very existence would' so it is stated, 'engender confidence in all Cypriots.' Indeed, the very existence of the U.N. Commissioner would have to be sufficient for this purpose, because Galo Plaza advocated the abrogation of all Treaties of Guarantee, and under the U.N. Charter no United Nations force or official may enter a country without the consent of its Government.

After having produced inadequate guarantees for the Turkish minority, the Galo Plaza Report went on to persuade the Greeks to voluntarily give up enosis. In support of this suggestion he put forward the arguments, from the British Colonial Period, that Cyprus and Greece have different systems of law and that Cyprus enjoys a higher standard of living.

The result of these efforts was that on 2nd February 1966, Makarios and the Greek Government declared that any proposed solution excluding enosis would not be acceptable. The Turkish reaction was more fundamental: The Ankara Government simply rejected Galo Plaza as Mediator. This was the end of U.N. mediators in Cyprus. The main points of the Galo Plaza Report were:

1. Cyprus should remain an independent State and should voluntarily renounce its right to choose union with Greece.

2. The island should be demilitarized, the question of the British sovereign bases being left aside for further consideration.

3. There should be no partition or physical separation of the Greek and Turkish communities, but Turkish Cypriot rights should be guaranteed by the United Nations and supervised by a United Nations Commissioner in the island.

4. A settlement must depend in the first place on the agreement between the people of Cyprus themselves and talks should take place between the Greek and Turkish Cypriots.[24]

It can be seen from above that, although Galo Plaza was completely wrong in his sociological analysis of Cypriot society and careless in his study of the 1960 Constitution, his proposals have body and soul because they see no possible future for Cyprus except as a united entity. Partition is condemned outright and the recommended talks between the two communities have become a reality and, at the time of writing the chief hope for a peaceful and equitable solution of the Cyprus problem depends on them. In this respect all those who desire the best possible settlement for Cyprus should give serious consideration to the outlines of this Report, particularly as the Turkish action of 1974 has clearly demonstrated the evils which Galo Plaza ascribed to partition and the uprooting of populations.

In the meantime, the Americans were alarmed at the thought that Cyprus might become a kind of Mediterranean Cuba. At the request of President Johnson, Mr. Dean Acheson, a former Secretary of State, arrived in the Summer of 1964 in Geneva and presented a Plan[25] to the Greek and Turkish Governments. Acheson proposed the following:

1. The union of the island with Greece.
2. The cession to Turkey of Costellorizo (a small island lying close to the Turkish coast).
3. The establishment of a Turkish military base on the Karpas Peninsula in north-eastern Cyprus.
4. The formation of two cantons under Turkish Cypriot administration, and,
5. The payment of compensation to Turkish Cypriots wishing to emigrate.

'The Plan was thoroughly unrealistic, for even if the Greek Government were to accept it, the Greek Cypriot never would. Indeed, the Plan would have had to be imposed on Cyprus by the force of Greek arms.'[26] Strengthened now by the election in Greece of a friendly and democratic Government, headed by the late George Papandreou, Archbishop Makarios wasted no time in consigning the Acheson Plan to the waste-paper basket.

On the Turkish side in Cyprus the most significant event, after the failure of the various proposed Plans, took place on December 29th 1967, when the Turkish Cypriot leaders announced the formation of a 'Transitional Administration.' Dr. Kuchuk now became President of this Turkish administration and R. Denktash, Vice-President. The representation of the U.N. Secretary-General managed to institute direct talks between the two communities. The Representatives met for the first time at the beginning of June 1968, and on the 24th June the Intercommunal Talks started officially with the

Special Representative in Cyprus for the U.N. Secretary-General, Mr. Osorio Tafall, as Chairman. Mr. Glafcos Clerides represented the Greek side and Mr. Raouf Denktash the Turkish side. The object of these talks was to find a solution for the island's problem. Unfortunately, as in similar situations of the post-1945 period, these talks have turned out to be very much like 'talks about talks', producing no practical results whatsoever. In the light of subsequent events, these talks, were only a smokescreen for the real Turkish tactics. Whatever went on at them, the basic Turkish objective was always a territorial partition of Cyprus. It is obvious that Makarios and his advisers came to the conclusion that time was on their side. For the Turks, on the other hand, the talks were far from futile because they knew that time was really on their side. The truth is that the Turks were consolidating their enclaves with the aid of mainland Turkey, while on the Greek side political fractioning was taking place owing to rival leaderships, confusion about enosis and the doubt sown by the military coup of 21st April 1967 in Greece. The Turkish contingent stationed in Cyprus under the Treaties remained on the island, garrisoned in the main Turkish enclave. The idea of the intercommunal talks, therefore, was to reassure the Cypriot Greeks that the Turkish side was willing to sit down and talk. All the time, however, the Turks were watching for the first break in the Greek position in order to intervene and partition the island. Unfortunately, the mounting frustration on the Greek side due to the shipwreck of enosis and the failure to solve the Turkish problem, was obvious and caused split loyalty in the Greek ranks, as the assassination attempt on 8th March 1970 and subsequent events show. The Turkish invasion of July 1974 will prove to be a lasting monument to the futility of the inter communal talks and the bad faith of the Turkish side. The talks constitute a proof that the only aim of the Turkish leadership has always been the destruction of Cyprus and the deprivation of a large section of its Greek people of their land and property. Anglo-American policy and interests supported the Turks in their endeavour, while the attitude of the Greek governments made it obvious that Turkey could act in Cyprus almost with impunity.

PART B

IV
The Greek Coup and its Repercussions on Cyprus

While Cyprus was going through the agony of secession and occupation there was a deterioration of political life in Greece. There is no doubt that the weakness displayed by various Greek Governments over Cyprus undermined the prestige of politics in Greece. It is always assumed that it is better to negotiate rather than fight, and the present age has made certain peoples pay very dearly for it in the long run.[1] The crisis over Cyprus, with its anti-N.A.T.O. orientation via Makarios' non-alignment, together with the discovery of a left-wing plot in the army (the Aspida affair[2]) determined the hard line right-wingers in the Greek army to plot to establish a military dictatorship. On 21st April 1967, the army seized power in Greece and thus put an end to both parliamentary democracy and the Greek Monarchy.[3]

The new military regime in Greece began by being unfriendly about the Greek Cypriot President, Archbishop Makarios. At the same time, they sought a meeting with Turkey and discussed the partition of the island. 'The two Prime Ministers met at the Greek-Turkish frontier on September 9th. The talks were a complete failure, and the communiqúe was merely a collection of platitudes. But Prime Minister Demirel, upon his return to Turkey, disclosed the extent to which the talks had been a failure from the Greek point of view. He made it clear that Turkey had turned down the Greek proposal for enosis, and that it had insisted on the validity of the Zurich agreement, which, according to him, could be changed only by joint agreement of all the interested parties. This, in Demirel's opinion, would ensure that the international equilibrium, which had been guaranteed by the Treaty of Lausanne for the

Eastern Mediterranean region, would not be disturbed. Demirel's statements fell like a bombshell in Greece. Papadopoulos and the junta government had had a resounding defeat. From what is reliably known, however, Papadopoulos did not propose pure enosis to the Turks. He proposed union of Cyprus with Greece, along with the establishment of Turkish military bases on the island. In other words, he reiterated the Acheson proposal.'[4]

The Graeco-Turkish negotiations were rudely disturbed by the battle of Agios Theodoros,[5] November 15th 1967, which spread to the village of Kophinou, with its threat of war being raised again. However, American and N.A.T.O. intervention secured the withdrawal from Cyprus of all Greek and Turkish forces in excess of those provided by the Treaty of Alliance. It was on this occasion that the Greek Colonels were forced by Turkey to withdraw Grivas from Cyprus too. Papandreou describes the whole affair as follows: 'The conclusion is inevitable that the incident had been arranged by Grivas on the junta's—Papadopoulas' orders, unbeknown to Collias. This treachery required a scapegoat. Grivas was selected for this role, and he was allowed to return to Cyprus. He was dismissed and later put under house arrest.'[6] The right-wing leanings of the Greek junta and its hasty compliance with the Turkish demands[7] were a great blow for the Government of Archbishop Makarios because he could no longer count on Greek support. This soon turned into enmity, as enosis ceased to be attractive and, for the new Greek regime, came to mean partition. This attitude of the Greek regime forced Makarios to make a speech on 12th January 1968, in which he stated that due to prevailing conditions, a realistic reappraisal of the handling of the Cyprus problem was necessary and pointed out that a solution must be sought within the limits of what is feasible which does not always happen to coincide with what is desirable.

This pronouncement by the President of Cyprus seems, in the changed circumstances, to have marked his sincere conversion to the cause of independence. However, this new approach earned Archbishop Makarios the final enmity of the extreme right-wing elements among the former E.O.K.A. fighters. Their enthusiasm for enosis seemed now to embrace the possible partition of the island or at least handing Turkey some base. For the new military regime of Greece enosis meant the achievement of the best possible relationship with Turkey and the U.S.A. Makarios stood in the way of such a settlement, therefore, it is not surprising that in 1970 an assassination[8] attempt was mounted against Makarios and the veteran George Grivas returned in September 1971, for the second time, to Cyprus and went into hiding. But this time his objective was a conspiracy against Makarios. The strife in Greece had fractured the Greek Cypriot front. The Greek Cypriots were now prevented from appealing to Greek public opinion due to the suppression of political freedom and the press. Even before 1967, Makarios and the late George Papandreou defeated various attempts against the integrity of Cyprus contained in the Acheson Plan and prevented various other attempts by the Greek Governments to reach an understanding with Turkey at the expense of Cyprus.

After the first assassination attempt[9] of 8th March 1970, Athens and Nicosia were no longer speaking the same language and Grivas remained in the background. It was obvious that the Greek regime had arrived at some understanding with Turkey to solve the intercommunal problem. Mr. John Bullock, the *Daily Telegraph* Correspondent, said: 'Greece who had clearly planted Grivas as a time bomb ticking away in the Archbishop's back garden, had reached a quick understanding with Turkey, her N.A.T.O. partner, that a settlement of the intercommunal problem in Cyprus should be arranged.'[10]

An additional source of friction between Makarios and Athens arose from the Archbishop's already outlined policy of non-alignment and his cultivation of friendly relations with the Soviet Union. Since 1964 Makarios had striven to obtain the support of the Soviet Union against any Turkish military threats, and he had been successful in purchasing arms from the Soviet Union and Czechoslovakia. The Archbishop visited Moscow in the Spring of 1971, and ever since then he has been subject to propoganda attacks in the right-wing Greek press that he was a communist and a red Archbishop.[11] It is to be recalled that even at the height of the E.O.K.A. struggle,

Makarios had been consistently accused by British and Turkish sources for being a front for a communist takeover of Cyprus. All this amounted to was that with the junta in power, pursuing its pro-American and N.A.T.O. policies, Cyprus was forced to look, and rightly so, elsewhere for support, as the position of Greece against Turkey weakened under the dictatorship from year to year.

The most startling feature of this period was the mounting barrage of accusations that Makarios was the enemy of enosis. This was the line pursued by the Greek military regime and their right-wing hangers-on in Cyprus. The most significant aspect of this move was that the military regime in Greece meant by enosis the achievement of a common front with its N.A.T.O. ally, Turkey. To this end, if necessary, Cyprus was to be partitioned between the two powers. Any resistance on the part of the Cypriots to preserve the unity of their island was now branded as anti-enotism and anti-hellenism, and Makarios was immediately subject to attack on this score. As the chief endeavour of Makarios through thick and thin has always been to preserve the unity of Cyprus, he would do hardly anything else in the circumstances than turn against the idea of enosis, as propagated by the Athens Colonels and to opt for independence—an independence to preserve the unity of Cyprus—as being the best hope for his country. But in the eyes of Athens such a course made Makarios look like a traitor to the cause of Hellenism. Makarios himself declared, on 12th January 1968:

'The Cyprus problem has entered a critical stage, the two main factors which contributed to this development were the failure of the Graeco-Turkish dialogue and the recent withdrawal from Cyprus of the Greek forces. I do not consider this time as appropriate for expressing views or making comments on these two events. I shall only refer briefly to the present position of the Cyprus problem and the line of policy which necessity dictates in the present circumstances.

'The failure of the Graeco-Turkish dialogue and the decision of the Greek Government regarding the withdrawal of the Greek forces stationed in Cyprus for over three years, have created circumstances and conditions dictating a realistic reappraisal of the handling of the Cyprus problem.

'I am aware that, owing to the recent unfavourable developments, there is an atmosphere of uncertainty and concern among the Greek Cypriots, and the question which is uppermost in their minds is as to the future course and the prospects of a feasible solution.

'I have repeatedly stated in the past that we desire to live in Harmony with the Turks of Cyprus. We do not wish to deprive them of their rights as equal citizens, far less do we aim at their extermination. On the contrary, we are prepared to grant to the Turkish Cypriots additional privileges. This intention we communicated some time ago to the Secretary-General of the United Nations.

'I consider it necessary on this occasion to stress that the Constitution of an independent and unitary State should be governed by democratic principles, be approved by the people and be subject to amendment by democratic machinery, in accordance with the will of the people as a whole. That part, however, which will constitute the "Charter of Rights" of the Turkish community, will be entrenched. In the very near future a document will be drawn upon the above lines which could form the basis for discussion. It is possible that other texts may be presented by other sides. We do not exclude their discussion, the more so if such discussion and any talks take place within the framework of the "Good Offices" of the Secretary-General.

'In the meantime we will continue our efforts for the restoration of peace and normal conditions on the island. It is to be regretted that the Turkish Cypriot leadership, by its decision to establish a "Cyprus Turkish Administration", has prevented the extension of pacification measures to the whole of the island. The measures announced last week will be operative as from midnight tonight.

'Finally, I wish to announce a personal decision. The Cyprus question has now entered its most critical phase. Courageous decisions and important initiatives are required if we are to break the present deadlock. A solution must necessarily be sought within the limits of what is FEASIBLE, which does not always coincide with the limits of what is DESIRABLE. In these circumstances, I feel I cannot continue as President without renewal of the mandate of the people. I am not deserting in critical moments, nor am I abandoning the field in time of struggle. I have, however, reached the conclusion that the Cyprus people should be given the opportunity to pronounce on me and to express its will as to the handling of the Cyprus problem. I am not motivated by ambitions of a personal nature, nor by any personal or party interests. I am simply the servant of the people at a critical time, devoting all my efforts to their service and having the moral satisfaction of their love and confidence. If it is the view of the people that my services are inadequate, it may choose another leader. I am ready to submit to the will of the people expressed through elections.'[12]

The preoccupation of the military regime in Greece with maintaining a common front with Turkey and N.A.T.O. to the extent of downgrading the cause of enosis is not surprising in view of the history of Greece in the 20th century. It must be remarked that the era of Venizelos and Ataturk marked a turning point in respect of the Greek attitude towards Turkey. Turkey ceased to be considered as the national enemy number one. The Cyprus issue did not exist, and Venizelos and Ataturk had come to an equitable arrangement about Constantinople. On the other hand, a threat to Greece developed from the side of Fascist Italy. Greece was invaded by Italy and Germany during World War II, and the result of the axis occupation of Greece was a communist-led resistance movement. This movement was responsible for the Civil War in Greece which raged from 1944 to 1949, leaving lasting effects on the political life of the country. In addition to this, all the northern neighbours of Greece became communist states and initially dependent on Moscow. The victory of the anti-communist forces in Greece, with the help of the British, brought about a re-orientation of national attitudes. The enemy was now communism inside the country and the communist countries in the north. In contrast, Turkey had been neutral in World War II; its political life had never been disturbed by communist militancy and it did not feel itself as threatened as Greece was by its communist neighbours linking hands with dangerous forces inside the country. There was, therefore, no major re-orientation of Turkish attitudes. The Turks continued to regard the Greeks as enemies, and enjoyed the freedom of action which frightened Greece could not have. This fear of communism has been at the bottom of the poor diplomatic record of Greece over the Cyprus problem and the military regime in Greece felt that, as they were the champions of anit-communism, they had to get rid of the Cyprus problem at any price in order not to disturb their adjustment with Turkey and the U.S.A. This explains why the concept of enosis in the hands of the colonels changed its meaning entirely and could no longer be acceptable to Makarios.

In view of the above, Makarios became the chief obstacle to the entire policy of the Athens regime, and, if one considers the background of this regime, it is not surprising that very soon this regime came to devote all its energies to remove Makarios. To this end, they adopted a policy of engineering the assassination of Makarios, organizing an underground conspiracy against him in Cyprus, trying to undermine his position as Archbishop[13] and, finally all this having failed, they organized the ignominious coup of 15th July 1974.

After the failure to get rid of Makarios by assassination attempts, the Athens regime decided to send to Cyprus, as already mentioned, General Grivas in September 1971, to organize a terrorist campaign against the Makarios Government. Grivas began to organize a terrorist movement which became known as E.O.K.A.-B. This force mounted bomb attacks and raids on police stations and achieved a collaboration with the officers of the Greek contingent on the island. However, it must be pointed out that Grivas was placed in an extremely difficult situation. He was and he remained to the end of this life, 28th January 1974, an undeviating partisan of enosis. Although he had always disliked and mistrusted Makarios, he knew that the policy of the Athens regime was aimed at the partition of the island. As previously in his career, Grivas found himself in the position of a loner. He was an enemy of Makarios but he would not carry out blindly the policy of the Athens junta. Indeed, this does him credit. He spent the last years of his life in hiding, and, as long as he lived he did not engineer or permit any coup against the Archbishop. It seems that he had adopted a wait-and-see policy to remind the Archbishop that he was there providing an alternative, but he would not associate himself with the now openly pro-Turkish policy of the Athens regime. It has been rumoured recently that Grivas did not die a natural death, but had been poisoned by Greek officers who considered him a hindrance to their plans. Whatever the truth of this allegation, the fact remains that as long as Grivas was alive, no coup took place in Cyprus. In reality, Grivas' political influence both in Greece and Cyprus was nil. He was a great organizer, a most skilled guerrilla fighter, but politically he was always unsuccessful or, at least, negative,[14] The record of his last years in Cyprus show that he was incapable of achieving anything, and all he could do was to prevent and delay. It is still premature in the circumstances to prejudge the career and achievement of George Grivas. It can be said only that he was a singleminded, ruthless and honest patriot. History will have to judge the other aspects of his activities.

By 1974, all the attempts of the military regime in Greece to bring down Makarios had failed. Makarios was too popular with 99 percent of the Greek Cypriots to be brought down either politically or ecclesiastically, since he held both these offices through election by an enthusiastic popular vote. Yet, with the enigmatic Grivas dead, the Greek officers and E.O.K.A.-B. diehards decided to launch a direct coup against Makarios and his Government as, in their estimation, this was the only way to achieve success. In this way the military regime in Athens wanted to spread its methods to Cyprus. They had need of a desperate success abroad as things were not going too well at home. The original leader of the great coup, Colonel G. Papadopoulos, was under house arrest and his successors were aiming to cover up their divisions and inefficiency. The whole regime in Athens had already been shaken by a student revolt at the Polytechnic of Athens, the suppression of which proved to be a major military operation, costing more than a hundred lives. In the event, what was going to be their masterstroke in Cyprus, aiming at solving all their difficulties, came to be their own final undoing.

Misery and destruction after the invasion.

View of Famagusta before the invasion.

Famagusta after the invasion.

V
International Power Politics and Cyprus

It must be noted that in the history of post-colonialism, Cyprus is the only territory of the former British Empire which failed to gain complete self-determination. This exception is in itself highly significant. It is due, on reflection, to its geographical position. 'Cyprus has been the victim of geography for 3,000 years—and history has always lent a hurtful hand, too. This predominantly Greek island is only 50-odd miles from the Turkish mainland, but it is 600 miles from Athens. It may look only a speck on the map, but contemporary geo-political factors give it a strategic significance out of all proportion to its size.'[1] Cyprus forms part of the Middle East area which since the end of World War II has become the most neuralgic area of the World; owing to the fatal Arab-Israeli conflict, its tremendous oil resources and its dangerous economic and social structure all of which are endangered in Western eyes, by the geographical situation of the Soviet Union. This is why the Western powers, in reality the U.S.A., have a vital interest in the area. Their alliances must include the Eastern Mediterranean area in order to ensure their security not only in this area, but throughout the world. Both Greece and Turkey have been members of N.A.T.O. since 1951. Greece was one of the victor allied states of World War II and Turkey joined N.A.T.O. as an ex-neutral. The solidarity between these two nations is necessary for the success of the objectives of the Alliance in the area and, bearing in mind the vital importance of the area, perhaps for the Alliance as a whole. Therefore, any crumbling of the understanding between Greece and Turkey can have only disastrous results for the Western powers, especially the U.S.A. Cyprus has turned out to be a disturbing factor in

Graeco-Turkish relations and, thus of vital importance to the U.S.A. This explains the elaborate compromises and subterfuges which accompanied the end of the colonial regime, and which denied the completion of the principle of self-determination to the island. This had to be done in order not to upset the power structure and endanger the strategic interests of the powers.

One look at the map of the area shows that today the U.S.A. has succeeded Britain in keeping the power of Russia away from Constantinople, and the successors of Ataturk find themselves in a similar situation to their Ottoman predecessors and their protecting power, Britain. Turkey, in its geographic position, isolates Russia from the Eastern Mediterranean and the Persian Gulf area with its oil resources. Given the Arab-Israeli conflict and growing Arab hostility to the West, the vision of the Soviet Union advancing across Turkey to join hands with pro-communist movements in Arab countries is a nightmare because if this were to become a reality, the Western World would suffer a blow from which it might not recover.

The unique position of Turkey in respect of Russia not only gives it an advantage over Greece but practically over every other member of the N.A.T.O. Alliance. From the point of view of economic support and the supply of arms, all allies of the U.S.A. are in a position of dependents. This position of dependency applies particularly to such a country as Greece[2] and was much in evidence during the military regime in that country. Turkey, on the other hand, because it considers itself indispensable to Western interests, could always afford to pursue a more autonomous policy in the area, and this includes the Cyprus problem.

It goes without saying that for the Soviet Union any weakening of N.A.T.O. in the Eastern Mediterranean and any alteration in respect of Turkey were of vital interest. This explains the fact that the Soviet Union has paid considerable attention to Cyprus as compared to other ex-colonial territories. The geographical issues involved bring Soviet Russia into direct confrontation with the U.S.A. in the area and explain the reason why Cyprus has not been able to escape from the consequences of the international power political struggle and intrigues ever since it became an independent Republic and has had to pay a price for it. This is because a confrontation between Greece and Turkey must escalate into a confrontation among the major powers.

'Ethnic conflict between Greeks and Turks in Cyprus had led, and will lead inexorably in the future, to confrontation between Greece and Turkey. Britain, as a guarantor power is also immediately involved. All this in turn, gives rise to problems within the Western Alliance (N.A.T.O.) and automatically draws the United States into the picture. Intense U.S. and N.A.T.O. activity in the Eastern Mediterranean tends to bring about the reaction of the Soviet Union and the issue then reaches the level of World politics involving the stakes of war and peace.

'Finally, Cyprus' membership in the United Nations and her ties with the non-aligned nations bring an additional factor to bear on the power equation around this small island. This, in fact, has been the general pattern and complexity of international crisis over Cyprus since 1963-1964, in 1967, and again, in 1974.

'Considering this extremely complex network of conflicting interests involving Greece, Turkey, Britain, the United States, N.A.T.O, the Soviet Union, the United Nations, and, most important of all, the divided people of Cyprus, the only way of reconciling most of these interests is to maintain and preserve a truly independent democratic Cyprus. Viewed in this perspective, the Greek junta's engineered coup in Cyprus in July was a clear attempt to impose an unacceptable solution. So too, however, was the military intervention of Turkey which now threatens partition.'[3]

'From the American point of view, the crucial thing about the quarrel was not the rights and wrongs of the two communities on the island, but the damage it did to relations between Greece and Turkey, both allies of the United States. If the two countries went to war over Cyprus, the security of American bases in both countries would be undermined. Moreover, both countries would be using weapons provided by the United States, as indeed they already were. (This, of course, represented the "reductio ad absurdum" of the military-centred foreign policy which the United States had been following, and of the assumption that "anti-communism" was an adequate foundation for a military alliance). What mattered, therefore, was not the basis on which a solution was reached; it was simply the surmounting of the immediate crisis. The "Acheson Plan" for a partition of Cyprus was regarded by many Greeks as part of a sinister plot for the extension of American power at the expense of the rights of the Greek Cypriots. But in all probability, it was simply the same sort of knee-jerk reaction that has caused advocates of "Realpolitik" to resort to partition—usually with disastrous results—as a "solution" to communal tensions elsewhere. It was, in any case, less important in American eyes than the steps to defuse the immediate situation. These included the imposition of a truce, the establishment of a U.N. force to supervise it, and the prevention of a Turkish invasion of the island. Such measures certainly helped to preserve the N.A.T.O. alliance and the American military position in the Eastern Mediterranean by temporarily papering over the Greek-Turkish conflict. But they also averted a war which would have been disastrous for the people of the area. Their accomplishment did nothing to secure a permanent solution of the Cyprus problem, and it left both Greeks and Turks resentful; each side felt that the United States had betrayed it by not giving it unlimited backing against the other. On the whole, the Turkish resentment was probably greater because most Turks felt that without international intervention they would have been able to "solve" the Cyprus problem by force of arms. One result was a significant re-establishment of harmonious relations between Ankara and Moscow. But there was enough resentment in Greece to exacerbate still further the tensions which existed in Greek-American relations."[4]

The emergence of an independent Cyprus with its uneasy communal situations soon convinced the U.S.A. that this was a factor which could produce an armed conflict between her allies, Greece and Turkey. Such a conflict as outlined above, would prove fatal to the Western World and had, therefore, to be averted at all costs. The fatal nature of the conflict so the Americans felt, could be enhanced by the direct involvement of the Soviet Union. For this reason, American policy could not regard Archbishop Makarios with favour. In their eyes he was a destroyer of harmony, fanatically bent on setting Greece against Turkey in order to achieve his ultimate aim of enosis.

From a N.A.T.O. point of view, such an estimation of Archbiship Markarios is indeed correct. He has throughout his career paid secondary attention to international entanglements, concentrating solely on the liberation of his homeland, for the sake of which he is willing to exercise a choice of policies and allies. This has made Makarios a pure nationalist in the classical sense and a stranger to the type of world taken from the Pentagon, and from the U.S.A.'s point of view he has been a threat to them. Consequently, American policy, being mainly committed to Turkey, has on the whole been hostile to the policy of the Archbishop, both in respect of enosis and the full independence of Cyprus.

In this situation, faced by American and N.A.T.O. hostility, Makarios had no option but to embark on a course of non-alignment foreign policy and above all, established friendly relations with the Soviet Union and the Arab countries. This policy seemed at first to pay off during the crisis of 1964, when both the U.S.A. and the Soviet Union restrained Turkey from invading[5] Cyprus. The then Soviet Government led by the late Mr. Khruschev, announced that in the case of a foreign invasion of Cyprus the Soviet Union would help the Republic to defend its freedom and independence. It is no wonder that immediately after the 1964 crisis, the U.S.A. launched a major diplomatic plan to resolve the Cyprus problem. It was now that the U.S.A. proposed the Acheson Plan, already fully described, and the rejection of it by Makarios further annoyed the U.S.A. Government who were already pre-disposed against the Archbishop's Government. The same fate was suffered by the effects of Cyrus Vance, special envoy of the President of the U.S.A., in 1967, when Makarios refused to abandon the U.N. approach to the solution of the Cyprus problem in favour of a N.A.T.O. one.

For the Soviet Union the Cyprus issue constituted an effective means for weakening the southern flank of N.A.T.O., and this objective has persisted throughout all the twists and turns of this policy. The policy was aimed at an aggravation of Graeco-Turkish relations and loss of faith and confidence in the U.S.A. by either Greece or Turkey, or both[6]. In this respect, following the crisis of 1964, when the Turkish Government began to cultivate better relations with the Soviet Union, the Russians began talking of the 'two communities' of Cyprus, and began to examine the merits of federation as a possible solution. It can be seen that the balance of power between Greece and Turkey was very closely observed by the Soviet Union. After the military coup of 1967, the Soviet Union concluded that Greece was now the favourite of the U.S.A. and its policy began to favour Turkey and this phase lasted until the invasion of Cyprus, 15th July, 1974. Whether this policy of setting Greece and Turkey at each other will bring about the collapse of the N.A.T.O. front in the Eastern Mediterranean, remains to be seen. The Soviet Union would prefer not to risk a confrontation with the U.S.A. However, it wants to derive all the possible advantages from a Graeco-Turkish conflict. Finally, it emerges from the Soviet approach to the Cyprus problem, that the Soviet Union is not in the least interested in the settlement of the internal constitutional problem as long as Cyprus remains non-aligned, and a non-militarized island.

The events leading to the invasion of Cyprus by Turkey in July 1974, had their external as well as their internal causes. The internal causes have already been analyzed to some extent. The external causes should now become more apparent, and must be put down entirely to the fatal consequences which the military regime in Greece has had on the external relations of their country. The dependence on the U.S.A., which was the road chosen by the military rulers of Greece, convinced the American Government that the subservient military dictatorship in Athens would not react to any Turkish move over Cyprus, and it felt that its interest would be best served by granting greater favour to Turkey. For this reason, there was no need for an attempt by the U.S.A. to restrain Turkey in 1974, as they did in 1964.[7] At the same time, the Soviet Union too, because of the regime in Athens, adopted an anti-Greek attitude. These factors in the external situation, constituting for the time being a virtual agreement between the super powers enabled Turkey to act in 1974 as she had not been able to act in 1964. The resulting invasion of Cyprus demonstrates the fact that the Cyprus problem is now of international dimensions. Unlike the Arab-Israeli problem, both N.A.T.O. countries and the super powers are directly engaged. Greece has regained her freedom of action and thus the U.S.A. can no longer afford not to pay heed to the Greek point of view. This might induce the U.S.A. to pressurize Turkey to be more reasonable rather than risk at best a breakdown of the Eastern flank of N.A.T.O. and at worst a world conflict.

VI
The Invasion and Drama of Cyprus

1974 was the fourteenth year of the independence of Cyprus, and the tenth year of the Turkish succession. The position of the Archbishop was becoming precarious. The regime in Greece was very unfriendly, and an efficient terrorist organization, E.O.K.A.-B., was preparing the ground for some drastic action. One should not be deceived by the fact that the vast majority of the Greek population of Cyprus was loyal to Archbishop Makarios and, moreover, the majority was reaping great economic benefits from the growing prosperity of the country. The terrorist organization, being masterminded by Grivas, was very small but as efficient as anything that Grivas could have produced. What made the organization more deadly for Makarios and his Government was the fact that it was in liaison with the Greek officers who in addition to commanding the Greek contingent stationed in Cyprus under the Treaties, were also in control of the Cypriot National Guard. This put Athens in a good position to seize control of Cyprus. It was probably Grivas himself who had stood in the way of such a move, but with Grivas' death Athens was free to get rid of Makarios once and for all. The Archbishop felt threatened by the presence of the Greek officers in Cyprus and wrote a letter,[1] on 2nd July 1974, to the then President of Greece, General Ghizikis, demanding their removal from the island.

On Saturday, 6th July 1974, Archbishop Makarios made public the contents of this letter to General Ghizikis:

'I am sorry to say, Mr. President, that the roots of the troubles are very deep, and they stretch from Athens. The Tree of Evil is nurtured and grows there . . . To spell it out in more precise terms, I would say that the higher echelons of the military Regime in Athens, support and direct the activities of the terrorist organizations, known as E.O.K.A.-B. This explains the participation of the officers of the National Guard in the illegal acts and the conspiracies... Documents recently discovered and seized from E.O.K.A.-B. leaders prove this... I cannot say that I hold a particularly warm place in my heart for military regimes and particularly for that of Greece, the cradle of democracy... I have often felt—and even brushed against—the invisible hand that reaches out from Athens to wipe me out....'[2]

Just three days before the coup of 15th July 1974, the Archbishop asserted that he had convincing evidence that the Colonels[3] of Greece were plotting his overthrow. Yet Makarios could not believe that the Greek officers would dare to stage a coup within such a short space of time. But on 15th July, at 8.30 a.m., the blow fell and an attempt to assassinate the Archbishop was made, and the Presidential Palace was demolished. The *News Week* correspondent, Mr. M. R. Benjamin, reporting on the fighting says:

'At exactly 8.30 a.m., the rebels awaited signal, the shriek of a factory siren, echoed across Nicosia. The coup was starting right on time. Tanks and trucks filled with soldiers began racing through the narrow streets of the Cypriot capital. Ten Soviet-made T-54 tanks formed a semi-circle around the front of the yellow sandstone Presidential Palace—which Makarios had entered a half hour before... They opened fire. Outnumbered and outgunned, the police guarding the Palace nevertheless held their ground. For three hours, the T-54's stood back and pounded the stately old building, confident that Makarios was trapped inside. But in the first minutes of the attack, the Archbishop—accompanied by three body-guards—had slipped out a secret door into the garden in the back. They stepped into the road and flagged down an approaching car. As four armoured vehicles rounded a distant corner, the driver of the commandeered car made a U-turn, and the Presidential party sped away towards Paphos...'[4]

The Archbishop himself described to the author at the Grosvenor House Hotel on 26th November 1974, what happened:

'I had just returned from Troodos and I was greeting a delegation of Greek Orthodox schoolchildren from Cairo. It was about 7.45 a.m. Suddenly I heard a noise, something was repeatedly hitting the Palace. I realized what it was and I asked for the children to be removed to a safer place. I then decided, accompanied by my three bodyguards, to duck out of a rear door, crossed the garden where no tanks or armoured cars had yet appeared, and commandeered a passing car. As I lay on the floor, we drove to a village outside Nicosia, Klerou, where we stopped at the police station. We were offered coffee and the police sergeant gave us his car and we drove to the monastery of Kykko. In the meantime, the Cyprus Broadcasting Corporation was announcing "Makarios is dead! Makarios is dead!" When I arrived at the monastery, the people could not believe their own eyes. I stayed at the monastery for a while and then left with my three bodyguards for Paphos via my birthplace, the village of Panayia. I arrived at the Metropolis of Paphos and from a transmitter I spoke to my people declaring that I was alive and urging them to defend their country, freedom and democracy. At first I decided to make my stand in Paphos. I was advised that such a stand would be futile as a two-pronged pincer of National Guard armour and troops closed in on the town. I considered that outside I would be able to help my people more effectively in their struggle. I asked help from the U.N. contingent in Paphos and I was flown by helicopter to the British base from where I was flown in an R.A.F. 'plane to Malta. I stayed the night in Malta, and the next day I arrived in London. The next day I flew to New York where I put the case of my country to the world.'[5]

Meanwhile in Nicosia the Greek officers who had carried out the coup began putting out reassuring statements and installed a former journalist Nicos Sampson, as President. Sampson declared that nothing was changed, especially in the sphere of foreign policy, and that the intercommunal discussions, that had been going on for six years between Glafcos Clerides and Raouf Denktash, were to continue. When Sampson appeared on the television screen on 16th July 1974, he declared:

1. That Cyprus would remain an independent and sovereign State;

2. That the Foreign Policy of non-alignment would be maintained;

3. That the rights of the Turkish Cypriot community would be respected and that they had nothing to fear from a dispute which only concerned the Greek Cypriots.

The next major move was made by the Turkish Cypriots. The Turkish leader, Mr. R. Denktash, refused to recognize Sampson as President and called on Turkey and Britain to oppose him under the Treaty of Guarantee. The Turkish Government decided then and there that this was a golden opportunity to settle the Cyprus problem once and for all to their complete satisfaction. They decided to profit both from the international unpopularity of the Greek military regime as well as from the fact that Athens was now too much in the pocket of the U.S.A. to carry any weight with the State Department; they knew that the regime in Athens was so devoted to American interests that they would never question something which America approved of. Furthermore, it must be realized that owing to the international reputation of Makarios, Ankara would have thought twice about military action in Cyprus with the Archbishop still there. The Sampson regime[6] carried no weight with them, and a military adventure in Cyprus could be presented to the world as a virtuous action under the Treaties of Guarantee to restore the Constitutional status quo, i.e. Makarios and his Government. In the event Turkey failed to observe the Treaty of Guarantee by failing to consult the Greek regime, which it insisted on. However, given the contempt which even the Turks must have felt for the regime in Athens, and their ultimate intention to partition Cyprus, they could not have been expected at that time to observe all the niceties required by diplomatic practice. Their intention was to strike while the iron was hot, and strike they did.

On July 20th, 1974, a Turkish expeditionary force landed near Kyrenia, supported by parachute drops inside the main Turkish enclave established there since 1964, and by a naval and air bombardment, particularly of Nicosia airport. By 22nd July, the Turkish expeditionary force had taken over the town of Kyrenia and the entire Turkish enclave north of Nicosia including the 'Green Line' Turkish part of Nicosia itself. In this way, Turkey seized the most strategically important Turkish enclave in Cyprus, established in 1964, enlarged it by the seizure of Kyrenia, and joined it to the Turkish quarter of Nicosia. At this point, the military regime in Greece collapsed; its unfortunate stooge in Cyprus, Nicos Sampson, called on Mr. Glafcos Clerides, President of the House of Representatives, to assume the leadership of the Government according to the 1960 Constitution. Meanwhile, the U.N. Security Council insisted on an immediate end to the warfare in Cyprus to which Turkey agreed. This was achieved by the appearance in New York of Archbishop Makarios who declared:

'I have come here to seek the support of the International Community in our struggle to save the independence, unity and territorial integrity of Cyprus. I am here in the cause of justice and freedom for a small member state of the United Nations. I bring to this Assembly the agony of the people of Cyprus for the survival of their country in freedom and dignity . . .

'The case of Cyprus is a test of non-alignment and beyond that a test case for the United Nations. If the United Nations fails to make Turkey respect the Charter and its resolutions the faith of the small countries in the United Nations will seriously be shaken.'[7]

The whole position was now complicated by the fact that the Turkish delegation claimed that the armed intervention was only intended to safeguard the independence, territorial integrity and the security of the Republic of Cyprus. The Turks even argued that their aim was to restore the legal Government of Archbishop Makarios and that they were acting completely within the terms laid down by the Treaty of Guarantee. It must be pointed out here that the Turkish Prime Minister at the time, Mr. Bulent Ecevit, had been to London, prior to the Turkish invasion, in order to consult the British Government with a view of Britain joining Turkey in fulfilment of her obligations under the Treaty of Guarantee. The absence of Greece, the third Guarantor power, enabled the British Government to decline the Turkish offer. To Britain,[8] although the Turks were not acting entirely within the terms of the Treaty, it appeared as though they were only aiming at the status quo. It is possible that Britain hoped for a situation whereby the U.N. should become responsible for the solution of the problem, thus enabling the harassed British Government, with its own troubles in Ulster, to escape from its legal, moral and historical responsibilities towards Cyprus and all its people. The U.N. Resolutions[9] of July 20th and July 23rd, as well as calling for a ceasefire in Cyprus, called upon the three guarantor powers to undertake immediate talks to discuss the situation. This was now possible due to the restoration of a Constitutional Government in Greece and the return to power of Mr. Constantine Karamanlis. The Foreign Ministers of Britain, Greece and Turkey met in Geneva on 25th July 1974.[10] In Cyprus, the true Turkish policy was revealed. Although Constitutional Government had been restored with Clerides assuming power, constant Turkish reinforcements were being poured into the Turkish bridgehead both by sea and air, and the bridgehead itself was being gradually expanded all the time.

Polys Modinos, a jurist of international repute and Deputy Secretary-General of the Council for Europe for a number of years, stated:

'There can be no doubt left regarding the true intention of Turkey. Resolution 353 adopted on 20th July, by the Security Council, urged all Governments to respect the independence and territorial integrity of Cyprus. It ordered the parties to "ceasefire"; it called for the immediate cessation of foreign military intervention and inter alia called upon Greece, Turkey and the U.N., to undertake negotiations without delay in order to re-establish peace in the region and the constitutional Government of Cyprus.

'The "ceasefire", acceded to by Turkey, was repeatedly violated by the Turkish Army which, over a period of ten days, occupied a large area surrounding Kyrenia, and was thus able to concentrate 40,000 men, heavy campaign equipment and more than 300 tanks there. Later events proved that Turkey's acceptance of the ceasefire on 20th July was nothing but a calculated trick.'[11]

On July 25th 1974, the Foreign Affairs Ministers of Turkey and Greece and the British Secretary of State for Foreign and Commonwealth Affairs met in Geneva to 'adjust and to regularize within a reasonable time, the situation in the Republic of Cyprus, on a lasting basis, having regard to the international agreement signed in Nicosia on 16th August 1960, and to Resolution 353 of the Security Council for the United Nations.'

On July 30th 1974, the three Ministers of the Guarantor powers signed an agreement in Geneva, providing the 'areas in the Republic of Cyprus, controlled by the opposing armed forces on 31st July 1974, at 22.00 hours (Geneva time) should not be extended.' This tripartite agreement, defined the security zones, settled the matter of the enclaves, provided for a staged and gradual reduction of the armed forces and decided that 'new talks were to begin on 8th August 1974, in Geneva.'

When the Conference was resumed on 8th August, the Turkish delegation began pressing for a federal solution of the Cyprus problem thus anticipating a territorial resettlement before such a solution would be implemented. On Tuesday 13th August, at eight minutes past eight, Mr. Gunes, the Turkish Foreign Minister, rejected a proposal by Mr. Clerides, that the Conference adjourn for 36 hours to allow him time to consult with his people. 'It was Munich all over again with a veritable diktat.'[12] The Turks were insisting on a federal system under which the Turkish Cypriots would have a separate administration in a zone covering 38 percent of Cyprus, and secondly for a Cantonal system under which the Turkish Cypriots would occupy several areas:

'1. The constitutional order of Cyprus would retain its bi-communal nature, based upon the co-existence of the Greek and Turkish Communities, within the framework of the sovereign, Independent Republic, whose territorial integrity was assured;

2. This constitutional order, appropriately revised through the active co-operation and the freely expressed consent of the two communities, shall be such as to ensure their enjoying a feeling of complete security;

3. The co-existence of the two communities shall be achieved by institutional agreements dealing with the division of powers and functions between the Central Government possessing competence over State Affairs, and the autonomous

communal administrations exercising their powers over all other matters within zones to be defined in accordance with the provisions of paragraph 5;

4. The structure of the Central Government will continue to be that of a presidential regime;

5. The Greek and Turkish Communal administrations will exercise powers and functions in the zones that include respectively the wholly Greek and Turkish towns; the communal authorities being empowered to group the municipalities. For the same purpose, the towns and villages of mixed populations shall be placed under the communal authority of that community to which the majority of the population of the village belongs:

6. Legislative authority over the respective communal administrations shall be exercised by the members of Parliament, with the Greek and Turks sitting in separate Councils for that purpose.'[13]

The negotiations broke down and on 14th August, the Turkish air force resumed bombing Nicosia, Famagusta and other towns and villages causing civilian deaths, destroying hospitals, schools, hotels, civilian buildings and killing even U.N. soldiers. By the 16th August, a strong Turkish army force started advancing towards Famagusta. After the occupation of this town Cyprus was cut in half, with the entire north-east of the island under Turkish occupation and with the line of demarcation running through Nicosia itself. Only after the Turkish army had achieved this did the Turkish Government agree to another ceasefire instigated by the Security Council. By this time 40 percent of Cyprus was under Turkish occupation and Turkey declared they were going to create within this area a separate Turkish state on the island, whether federated or not with the rest of the island. The boundary of the Turkish military occupation was the so-called Attila line, claimed for years by Turkey to be the true boundary between a Greek and a Turkish Cyprus.

The negotiations in Geneva revealed that the Turkish delegation were there not to negotiate but to dictate.[14] It declared that there was no margin for discussion and that partition must be accepted by the Greek Cypriots. Such an attitude was tantamount to asking the parties concerned to accept the partition of Cyprus, as already executed, by force, by Turkey, as a *fait accompli*. That this state of affairs came about was due to the fact that Turkey, as well as anybody else, could well afford to disregard the various Security Council Resolutions as these Resolutions lacked any means for their implementation. In such a situation, Turkey being the predominant military power in the area, could impose its own conditions in the absence of any counter-balancing display of power. The absence of Britain and Greece from the military scene gave a free hand to Turkey.

The federal Turkish argument should not be taken seriously. If Turkey meant by restoring 'the constitutional position in Cyprus', the partition of the island, partition could also lead to annexation. This should imply to Britain and Greece, that there can be no hope of any further negotiations with Turkey on the basis of the Treaty of Guarantee if Turkey continues to insist on partition and a federal solution. All the powers concerned must realize this and come to the conclusion that a new approach must be made to the problem as the Treaty of Guarantee has obviously failed.

From the very beginning, the Turkish military action in Cyprus has been ruthless and brutal. Whether this was deliberate or not, is not known. There is no doubt that the Turks have shown complete disregard for the 1949 Geneva Conventions and other rules of international laws for the conduct of war. Indeed, the Turkish Government informed the international Red Cross that their action was 'police action' and not war, and that they were not going to observe the Articles of the Geneva Convention relative to the Protection of Civilians and Prisoners of War. Thus, the Turkish attack was marked by indiscriminate bombing, shelling and shooting. However, the damage inflicted during the course of actual military operations was in itself insignificant when compared with the constant harassment and ill-treatment of the Greek Cypriot civilian population by the advancing Turkish forces.

The Turkish troops systematically looted and plundered the property of all Greek inhabitants encountered, and often shot on sight any Greek unfortunate enough to have been observed.

Furthermore, very often Greek civilians were deliberately rounded up and taken away either to be executed or deported, to detention camps in Turkey. It is also feared that nearly 50 percent of the members of the Cyprus armed forces who were captured by the Turks were killed by their captors. Foreign journalists were able to observe numerous instances where defenceless women and young girls were raped and families were separated.[15] Iain Walker, the *Sun*'s Reporter, wrote on 5th August 1974: 'For, while the peace talks went on, Turkish soldiers were killing and terrorising innocent civilians. The behaviour of these troops will shock the world. As they are in Cyprus in the name of Turkey, that nation must immediately take action against the animals that wear its uniform. If Turkey fails in this duty it will be stained with the same guilt as the Greek officers who set Cyprus alight again in the first place.' It was obvious that Turkish policy was to spare neither age nor sex but, even worse, was the deliberate policy of forced expulsion of all Greek Cypriots from their homes in the area seized by the Turkish forces in order to create a zone which they intended to turn into a Turkish Cypriot region. It is to be noted that the expulsion of the civilian inhabitants and the robbing of their property was not done in the heat of battle, but was the result of a deliberate policy of depopulation in line with the ideas of the Turkish leader, R. Denktash, who had declared that the Turkish population of Cyprus must have a part of the island entirely to themselves in order to feel safe. In addition to this policy of depopulation and uprooting, the Turkish authorities have been making efforts to settle[16] Turkish citizens from Turkey in their zone of Cyprus and transferring to them illegally the property seized from the expelled Greek Cypriots. This creates an entirely new situation, as it is an attempt to alter by force the demographic balance of Cyprus. It is an attempt to colonize Cyprus by Turkey with a possible view to a future annexation.

It would be a scandal and an affront to the whole world if a policy of colonial annexation was permitted by the Great Powers. As the Turkish Government had gone out of its way to describe their action in Cyprus not as war but as 'police action', it seems that Turkey has always regarded Cyprus as its own property and will continue to do so until this point is cleared up on an international level.

The drama of Cyprus has been caused by the inability of the military regime in Greece to tolerate the Government and policies of Archbishop Makarios who stood in their way and somehow prevented them from pursuing their reactionary obsessions. The next step was undertaken by the Turkish Government which most cynically disregarded the Treaty of Guarantee while making out that it was acting under it. Turkey had long been sharpening its teeth for Cyprus. The coup against Archbishop Makarios was too good an opportunity to be missed and the Ankara Government decided to boost its prestige by a programme of territorial expansion in order to divert its own people from the many shortcomings of modern Turkey. Turkey has been using the Turkish minority in Cyprus in precisely the same way that Hitler used the presence of German minorities in the small Eastern European countries he wanted to destroy and annex. The minorities were used as a foot-in-the-door and to deceive world opinion. In a similar fashion the Turkish minority in Cyprus at the instigation of the Ankara Government, pleaded before the world that the policy of the Greek majority was the extermination of the Turkish minority and hence the seizure of territory by that minority and the subsequent partition of the island was the only answer to the problem. To put it in a nutshell, Turkey had an answer ready and thus created the problem to fit it. The policy of Turkey towards Cyprus smacks more of Hitler than of Attila, after whom the Turkish plan has been named.

From the human point of view, however, the most lamentable aspect of the Cyprus drama is the fate of nearly 200,000 Greek Cypriot refugees[18] driven out from their homes and deprived of their property by the Turkish forces. 'To visualise the magnitude of the problem, one has to transpose the percentages to other countries: in the United States the equivalent would be 84 million uprooted, homeless refugees; in Britain 22 million; in Russia 98 million; in France 21 million; in Germany 25 million. And still one would not get a true picture for those are affluent countries far surpassing Cyprus in resources, economic and otherwise.'[17] The refugees' homes and farms and other property have been assigned to the Turkish inhabitants and settlers from Turkey. Their lives have now little meaning and their plight is something which can be better identified with more primitive times. The problem is rendered more acute by two factors. First, the comparative lack of resources in the Greek part of Cyprus to cope with the influx of 200,000 destitute people. Secondly, in a predominantly agricultural society, when most people are born, live and die in their native village, the wholesale uprooting of a population has psychological as well as physical effects, which no amount of material aid can compensate.

Here, perhaps, are the roots of another Palestinian problem which will poison relations between the Greek and Turkish communities on the island under any scheme of Government which allows for partition and its consequences, as partition and 'federalism' will prevent the return of the refugees to their rightful homes. The refugee problem alone makes the division of Cyprus into Greek and Turkish regions highly undesirable because it entails the seeds of a tragedy the consequences of which can be nothing short of catastrophic for the whole island. This brings the consideration of the Greek/Turkish Cyprus problem back to square one. No federal solution is possible due to the fact that there have never been clearly defined Greek and Turkish regions of Cyprus and thus such regions will have to be created by a forced displacement of population which, in turn, would make the lasting value of a federal solution highly problematic, if not unworkable. Robert W. Komer[19] says:

'The federal solution Turkey is calling for would make Cyprus only nominally independent. In reality it would be partitioned de facto into two quasi-states each protected by its guarantors. Moreover, this uneasy compromise would be pregnant with seeds of further trouble. It might only prove to be another of the temporary patch-up jobs which avert the immediate crisis but perpetuate the problem.'

PART C

VII
Economic, Social and Political Consequences

At the time of writing, the Turkish occupation forces are in control of 40 percent[1] of the total area of Cyprus. In this area there are 162 Greek and mixed villages comprising 32.1 percent of all the inhabited localities of the Republic. Needless to say, the Greek population of these localities have been forcefully driven out and are refugees. Before the invasion, the total Turkish population of Cyprus amounted to 18.4 percent of the total population of the Republic. The Turkish minority owned 12.3 percent of the total area of Cyprus, or 16.8 per cent of the total land in private ownership, most of it devoted to agriculture. This zone housed, before the invasion, 36.2 percent of the population, most of them Greek. The actual number of Greek Cypriots who have been expelled from this area has been estimated at 158,600; but the destruction caused by warfare in other parts of the island and the creation of a no-man's land along the ceasefire line has raised the number of Greek Cypriots who have been obliged to leave their homes to nearly 200,000 which is about 40 percent of the island's total Greek population.[2]

The Turkish occupied area includes some of the best farmlands in Cyprus, and constitutes 65 percent of the total cultivated land. It is responsible, together with other resources there, and with resources of adjacent areas, for about 70 percent of the total gross output of the island. In this respect, it must be stressed that many of the areas on the Greek side adjacent to the so-called Attila line traced by the Turkish occupants across Cyprus, have been adversely affected by this partition due to the interruption of irrigation, communications, markets, etc. by the artificially imposed barrier of the occupation.

Below is an attempt to show the catastrophic effects on the economy of the Republic as a whole:

	£
Damages of households belonging to Greeks	250,000,000
Moveable property	100,000,000
Loss of goods kept in warehouses	26,300,000
Plant production	18,000,000
Livestock	11,000,000
Livestock production	12,000,000
Tractors and other agricultural implements	7,500,000
Farm units	9,500,000
Industrial equipment	24,000,000
Stocks	6,000,000
Loss from production	50,000,000
Assets of the Electricity Authority	7,600,000
Loss of income	3,000,000
Mining industry	9,400,000
Tourism income	23,000,000
Loss of investment in tourist industry	110,000,000
Port installations	10,000,000
Aircraft	3,000,000
Roads	34,000,000
TOTAL	**£714,300,000**

The above figures represent the immense wealth of physical assets, resources and structures situated there in the form of hotels, hotel apartments, houses, factories, orchards, irrigated fertile land, mineral and quarrying resources, water resources and an unestimated value of tourist land.

The area occupied by the Turks comprises almost all the cereal producing Mesaoria Plain, the tobacco growing Karpass Peninsula, the Kyrenia district rich in citrus, olives and carobs and the fertile Morphou Plain with its high yield citrus groves. Moreover, the area is rich in water resources, as it contains the island's only two springs, Kythrea and Lapithos, which supply 60 percent of the water available for irrigation. Production originating from these areas in 1972 amounted to 18.5 million pounds or about 46 percent of total agricultural production. The main products were citrus fruits (80% of total citrus fruit production), cereals (79%), olives (45%), potatoes (25%), tobacco (100%), carrots (86%), other vegetables (32%), fodder crops (65%), etc. Livestock production of the area amounted in the same year to about 12 million pounds or 47 percent of the total for the island. It is estimated that the invading Turkish army seized about 280,000 sheep and goats, 1,400,000 poultry and about 12,000 head of cattle belonging to Greek Cypriots, not to mention 48,000 pigs. In addition to losses in production and agricultural capital stock, the continuation of the occupation of these areas will have adverse repercussions on exports and, therefore, the income derived from them. Agricultural exports from these areas in 1973 represented 60 percent of the total agricultural exports of the Republic and over 42 percent of domestic supply. Moreover, the loss of this agricultural output will prove to be a serious blow to local industry which has thus been deprived of its agricultural base.

Further serious damage which cannot be expressed in monetary terms is the destruction by bombing of an area of about 85 square miles of pinewood forests on the Troodos mountain which represents one fifth of the main state forests. It is estimated that 42.2 percent of the total growing stock of the area has been burnt. While the loss of timber and the cost of reforestation will amount to several million pounds, it will take more than fifty years to restore the forests to their pre-invasion state even if it were possible to achieve the impossible task of reforestating the whole area now. The total damage must be also considered from the point of view of the adverse effects on soil conservation and on the ecological balance.

A similar danger is threatening the citrus fruit industry in Cyprus. Lack of proper irrigation can destroy the delicate citrus trees and it will take about 10-12 years until new trees planted reach a reasonable fruit bearing age. This danger to the citrus fruit industry is considerable because due to the expulsion of the Greek population there is not enough Turkish labour, nor do the Turks possess the experience necessary for this task.

In the field of the manufacturing industry, it is estimated

that factories situated in areas controlled by the Turkish army employed 32 percent of the manufacturing labour force and produced 26 percent of the manufactured production of Cyprus worth about 25 million pounds per annum. Their industrial equipment has been valued at 24 million pounds and in addition there were stocks totalling about 6 million pounds. These industries, now in Turkish hands, include meat preparation and dairy industries, export orientated plants in Famagusta and Morphou, grain milling and biscuit factories, the major oil and vegetable oil plants, carob kibbling and fodder factories, textile, footwear and clothing plants, almost all brick manufacturing plants and some mosaic plants, the entire lime producing plants, the only steel pipes plant and the plastics industry in Famagusta. The Nicosia industrial estate, an important concentration of industries equipped with the most modern machinery, all established since 1966, is now in Turkish hands and most of the plant has been shipped to Turkey. It is estimated that in 1973 this important industrial concentration of 60 modern, fast growing and efficient units had reached an annual production of 3.5 million pounds and was employing 1,000 people. Important textile clothing and footwear, flooring, paper sacks, foundry and turbine pump units were all reaching the stage of major expansion. Near the Nicosia industrial estate and along the Famagusta road up to the Kythrea/Kyrenia junctions, there are 26 major industrial units with outputs of about £1.4 million annually, and with three quarters of their output serving the construction industry, their closing makes the problem of reconstruction difficult. The closing of the important lime producing industries around Kythrea will make this problem even more acute. Altogether, exports of manufacturing products (other then processed agricultural products) will be adversely affected by 50 percent.

The mining industry, based on copper and asbestos was a major earner of foreign currency and made an important contribution to the Government's revenue. The quarrying sector was supplying the booming construction industry with the necessary raw materials. The Turkish invasion has severely disrupted activities in this important sector. The most important copper mine at Mavrovouni responsible for 60 percent of the total ore output as well as the quarries at Pentadaktylos are now under Turkish control. Out of a mining and quarrying output of £17 million in 1973, £9.4 million or 56 percent of the total originated from areas which are now under Turkish control. Mineral exports from those areas amounted to 42 percent of all mineral exports and 10 percent of the domestic supply. Moreover, the damage is augmented by the extra cost of shipping minerals from ports other than the Karavostassi/Xeros complex which was developed as the shipping centre for mining products.

Another gravely affected sector is the transport and communication sector. The Turks have seized the deep water port at Famagusta which handles 83 percent of general cargo, as well as the already mentioned specialized mineral jetty at Karavostassi. Also the Kyrenia yacht harbour, with its foreign exchange earning capacity, has been conquered by the invading forces. Larnaca harbour has been declared by the Turks a war zone and cannot easily be used for navigation. The loss of Famagusta port is the most grievous blow to the economy of the island as it alone represented over 50 percent of the total port capacity in Cyprus. Being for many years the main port of Cyprus, there is a high concentration of facilities worth many millions of pounds. All in all, total assets of ports in Turkish hands are estimated at about £10 million, of which the ore jetty at Karavostassi represents over £2 million. This does not include goods waiting customs clearance at warehouses and other goods valued at many millions of pounds in bonded or other authorized warehouses at Famagusta. The Nicosia international airport, which was the main airport in Cyprus, was the main target for the Turkish air attacks, and it has been put out of operation. Airport equipment and airline installations belonging to private companies have been heavily damaged. The main fleet of the Cyprus aeroplanes have been destroyed or put out of action. The loss of income resulting from the unused airport was estimated at over £4 million, at the end of 1974. The closure of the airport has cut off air transport and is causing serious economic damage to exports. The loss of revenue to the Government from the closing of the airport amounts to about £90,000 per month.

Internally, the Turkish invasion has disrupted the road network making efficient movement of people and goods difficult. The Turkish occupied area contains 43 percent of the roads. The loss of thousands of private cars and lorries cannot be estimated.

In the services sector, assets to the value of £7.6 million, belonging to the Electricity Authority of Cyprus are now situated in the occupied area. Nearly 60,000 consumers have been lost, representing a loss of revenue to the Authority of £2.7 million per annum. Also the Cyprus Telecommunications Authority has suffered much damage and a considerable proportion of its property lies in areas occupied by the invaders. The property of the Authority now in Turkish hands represents a value of £4 million, or 26 percent of the Company's total asset value.

Tourism in Cyprus was one of the fastest growing sectors of the economy, and Cyprus had recently become a tourist resort of international repute. In 1973, tourism accounted for £23.6 million in foreign exchange earnings and provided employment for about 10,000 people. Investment in tourism has been considerable. The value of capital assets was around £81 million in hotel accommodation and £30 million in ancillary facilities. Under normal conditions tourism was expected to fetch by 1974 over £30 million in foreign exchange, but as a result of the Turkish invasion £18 million was lost during 1974. It will take many years before the industry recovers and the loss in terms of income cannot be less than £100 million. The target for 1976 was that foreign exchange earnings from tourism would have risen to about £42 million or 21 percent of total earnings on current account.

The area now occupied by the Turkish invading forces contains the two most popular tourist resorts, Kyrenia and Famagusta, which attracted more than 70 percent of tourists staying in hotels and had the greatest potential for future development. The area under Turkish control is rich in archaeological treasures and beautiful scenery responsible for 82 percent of tourist accommodation, 96 percent of tourist accommodation under construction, 73 percent of total investment in tourist accommodation and 40 percent of investment in ancillary tourist services. Together with agriculture, the loss of practically the whole tourist sector constitutes an irreparable loss.

In the sphere of social services, health and education have suffered serious setbacks. Two out of six major district hospitals (Famagusta and Kyrenia) with a total of 151 beds were abandoned to the invading forces with most of the equipment. More disrupting are the effects on the Rural Health Services with eight out of seventeen Rural Health Centres falling within the occupied area, and representing about 46 percent of hospital beds in that area. Furthermore, the island's largest hospital establishment, the psychiatric hospital, suffered extensive damage during the bombing. As well as all this there is the health problem of the refugees. With nearly 200,000 people living in camps, with no sanitary facilities or proper clothing, and mostly underfed, the public health situation creates tremendous problems with the possibility of outbreaks of serious endemic diseases.

Education has been most seriously affected by the Turkish occupation. A total of 171 Elementary Schools were situated in the occupied areas and a further 23 cannot operate as they are situated in the front line. More than 41 percent of Elementary School children totalling 26,000 have been displaced. Similar figures apply to pupils in Secondary education. More than 42 percent of the school buildings are either occupied or are unsafe for use by children. About 13,000 children or 37.5 percent of the total have been displaced. A similar fate has befallen many other technical and special schools in the occupied areas.

The most serious social problem has been the population upheaval. About 200,000 Greek Cypriots, 40 percent of the total Greek population, are now refugees. They are now concentrated mostly in camps, living under lamentable conditions, and facing serious problems of survival because of malnutrition, cold and hygiene hazards. According to official Government statistics, out of the refugee total 164,000 are in need of constant care and assistance, which requires at least £2 million per month from the Government.

The Turkish population of Cyprus, despite appearances and propaganda, has also been affected, socially and economically. It is now as uprooted as the Greek one. Moreover, given the area of the Turkish zone the present Turkish population is too small to make that area economically viable. In addition, they lack the sufficient skills to operate the highly specialized tourist, mining and agricultural (citrus growing) industries of the area. One way to solve this problem would be to introduce settlers from Turkey to ease the shortage of labour.[3] But such a settlement would prove the first and inevitable step towards the annexation of that part by Turkey. On the other hand, a federal solution for Cyprus without introducing settlers would fail as the Turkish sector of the federation could never become viable due to shortage of labour. Therefore, any separation of the two communities in Cyprus under any federal scheme must mean either the subsequent annexation of the Turkish part by Turkey, or its economic withering away, with woeful consequences for its population and their political leaders.

A political result of the Turkish invasion, whatever the precise settlement to be arrived at, must be that the Constitutional framework of the Republic (i.e. the 1960 Constitution) will have to be drastically revised. The invasion has finally destroyed both the constitutional structure of the Republic and its political framework. However, Cyprus is still an independent and sovereign State recognized internationally, and a member of the United Nations; and the Government of the Republic still exercises authority under the 1960 Constitution. Any political settlement of the issue will have to result in a new political structure. On the whole, the Turks insist on a rigid territorial separation and the Greeks favour a united solution. The principal objection to a territorial separation is that there has been a forced displacement of the population and the establishment of the Attila line. Thus, the Turkish action has, in a sense, been counter-productive to federation as it has created a situation which it is totally unacceptable to the Greeks, as emerged from the intercommunal talks, it would have been far easier for the Greek Cypriots to accept some form of the Turkish separate enclaves already existing, which had functioned for ten years. With the passage of time, the status quo might have become the desired solution which, it is believed, would have been acceptable to both communities. Unfortunately for both the communities of the island, the Turkish invasion, according to Senator Edward Kennedy, has 'turned the island into shambles. In political terms, it violated the integrity of an Independent State. In economic terms, it shattered the island's flourishing development. And in human terms, it turned half the population into refugees, detainees or beleaguered people caught behind ceasefire lines. A drive along the roads of Cyprus today quickly tells the tragic tale of the Cypriot people, of the human consequences of the armed invasion, or bombing and napalm, of ceasefire violation, of deadlock diplomacy, of military occupation and of war's inhumanity to man in the Turkish occupied areas of the north. Desolation and destruction are everywhere.'[4]

VIII
Solution or Dissolution

The problem that exists is a Graeco-Turkish problem. The fact remains that, once upon a time, the Turks ruled the entire Eastern Mediterranean, and all the Greeks, not only Cyprus were under their rule. Historically, the Greek cannot help resenting the Turk as a former oppressor and the Turk cannot help having contempt for their former subjects be they Greeks, Arab or Balkan Slavs. In Cyprus the despised Greeks are the majority of the population and economically have for a long time been literally the masters of the island. The Turkish minority has always been presented as the outnumbered and threatened race but, if the geographic situation of Cyprus is taken into account, Cyprus is an off-shore island of Turkey, and the Turks are in the majority if this area is taken as a whole, making the Greek Cypriots a tiny minority of about half a million virtually at the mercy of 39 million Turks. This aspect of the situation has been persistently ignored both by the detractors of the Greek Cypriots as well as by the Greek Cypriots themselves in their stubborn pursuit of enosis.

This pressure from the Turks has served to deprive the Greek Cypriots, as observed before, first of their aspirations to self-determination, and then of their independence and territory. It also means that the Turkish population of Cyprus has never considered itself to be a minority but a separate community enjoying the same rights as the numerical majority. This was due partly to their former status as masters and partly to the British policy during most of the colonial period. The only chance to create an integrated Cypriot personality existed during the early years of the British colonial regime when the policy of anglicising[1] the whole population was attempted.

Due to the resistance of the Greek element to such a policy the British abandoned it in favour of fostering separate Greek and Turkish communities in the spirit of the classical device of divide and rule.

At the time of the Radcliffe Proposals in 1956, the Turkish Cypriots demanded equal representation to that of the Greek Cypriot community. The criticism of such an attitude was voiced by Lord Radcliffe in his Report in the following words:

'I have given my best consideration to the claim put before me on behalf of the Turkish Cypriot community that they should be accorded political representation equal to that of the Greek Cypriot community. If I do not accept it I do not think that it is out of any lack of respect for the misgivings that lie behind it. But this is a claim by 18 percent of a population to share political power equally with 80 percent, if it is to be given effect to, I think that it must be made good on one or two possible grounds. Either it is consistent with the principles of a constitution based on liberal and democratic conceptions that political power should be balanced in this way, or on other means that the creation of such political equilibrium will be effective to protect the essential interests of the community from oppression by the weight of the majority, I do not feel that I can stand firmly on either of these propositions. The first embodies the idea of a federation rather than a unitary State. It would be natural enough to accord to members of a federation equality of representation in the federal body regardless of the numerical proportions of the populations of the territories they represent. But can Cyprus be organised as a federation in this way? I do not think so. There is no pattern of territorial separation between the two communities and, apart from other objections, federation of communities which does not involve also federation of territories seems to me a very difficult constitutional form. It it is said that what is proposed is in reality nothing more than a system of functional representation, the function in this case being the community life and organisation and nothing else. I find myself baffled in the attempt to visualise how an effective executive government for Cyprus is to be thrown up by a system in which political power is to remain permanently divided in equal shares between two opposed communities. Either there is stagnation in political life, with the frustration that accompanies it, or some small minority group acquires an artificial weight by being able to hold the balance between the two main parties. A third alternative, that the Governor should be given under the Constitution some sort of arbitral position as between the two communities, I have already excluded by what I have said above. I do not think that it will be advantageous to embroil the Governor in the internal controversies of the self-governing side. My conclusion is that it cannot be in the interests of Cyprus as a whole that the Constitution should be formed on the basis of equal political representation for the Greek and Turkish Cypriot communities.

'Does the second ground lead to a different result? I do not think so. To give an equal political strength in a unitary State to two communities which have such a marked inequality in numbers—an inequality which, so far as signs go, is as likely to increase or decrease—is to deny to the majority of the population over the whole field of self-government the power to have its will reflected in effective action. Yet it might well be right to insist on this denial if the Constitution could not be equipped with any other effective means of securing the smaller communities in the possession of their essential special interests. Not only do I think it can be equipped with such means by placing those interests under the protection of independent tribunals with appropriate powers and relying only to a limited extent on direct political devices, but I think that the "legalist" solution which this depends on is in fact better suited to provide the protection that is required, and it does not have the effect of denying the validity of the majority principle over a field much wider that that with which special community interests are truly concerned.'[2]

Following the Turkish succession of 1963, the Turkish Cypriots, as already pointed out, converted their demand for partition (Taksim) to a federal solution based on geographical separation. This demand for the territorial carving up of Cyprus was criticized by the U.N. Mediator Galo Plaza in his Report of March 1965:

'The arguments for the geographical separation of the two

communities under a federal system of government have not convinced me that it would not inevitably lead to partition and thus risk creating a new national frontier between Greece and Turkey, a frontier of a highly provocative nature . . .'

In the intercommunal talks, already referred to, the Turkish side shifted its position again from partition and federalism to complete separation between the two communities at every level creating a completely Turkish administration within the framework of a unitary state. This was the price that the Turkish community asked for, in return for their agreement to some of the 13 proposals of Archbishop Makarios and in particular to that dealing with the Vice-Presidential veto. It is to be recalled that the Turkish invasion of July 1974 resulted in the seizure of nearly 40 percent of the island thereby creating the separate Turkish zone. This having been achieved, the object of any negotiations, from the Turkish point of view, was to achieve an integration of this purely Turkish zone with the Greek zone under some form of federation. It is vital to observe that during all the previous talks about federation an exclusively Turkish area of Cyprus did not exist, but it would have had to be created. This time such an area has been forcefully created and federation with the Greek area is offered as the only solution. However, in addition to all the arguments against a federal solution in Cyprus emanating from Lord Radcliffe, Dr. Galo Plaza and Mr. G. Tornaritis, Attorney General of the Republic of Cyprus, as well as the obvious geographic and economic objections to it the fact remains, already discussed previously, that the Greek community will never accept the Turkish seizure of their part of Cyprus by force. If federation within the present context, as it exists in Cyprus, is to be rejected and rejected it must be, what would be the consequences and what solution is preferable to it?

Only the unitary nature of the island and the state in Cyprus can ensure the economic viability of the Turkish community itself and the territorial integrity of the state. Otherwise, the Turkish sector, instead of forming a part of the proposed federation, will gravitate to Turkey. It has been stated over and over again that in Cyprus, federation means partition and that only a strong and impartial unitary state can contain the two communities. Perhaps the ideal solution to the problem would be the creation of such organs of state through which both communities could work without the minority community feeling itself threatened with no territorial base.

The first requisite for such a settlement would be the return of the Greek refugees to their original homes and thereby the abolition of the Turkish area created by force.[3] In exchange for this, the Turkish community could be given enclaves larger than they held after 1963. These enclaves should no longer constitute ghettoes for the minority, but the base for areas of local self-government where the Turks would be in an unquestioned majority. There should be a devolution of the powers of the central government to the local authorities. Where the Turks would constitute the majority, local administration would be entirely in their hands. In mixed areas where Greek and Turkish villages adjoin each other or where there has been some return of the Turkish population to homes they occupied before 1963, the two communities should be represented in local administration in proportion to their numbers. Proportionate participation or representation by the two communities should apply to all services and organs of the state. The central government, in order to command the confidence of both communities, must be constituted at first as under the Constitution of 1960 but without the crippling veto. There is no harm in envisaging a time when the functions of the President of the Republic and Chief Executive would be separated. The President would then be merely the Head of State while the Chief Executive would concentrate the political power and, as the Greek element would constitute the majority, it is to be expected that he would be a Greek Cypriot, but, on the other hand, the President of the Republic could be Turkish representing all the Cypriots.[4] Such a constitutional arrangement would constitute a bi-communal though unitary state. The communal aspect of the state would find its full application in local affairs and those affairs already assigned by the Constitution of 1960 to the Communal Chambers, the scope of which should be augmented except in the spheres of taxation. No necessary provisions should be made for the creation of separate Turkish municipalities as it is presumed that in those municipalities (enclaves) where the Turkish population would form a majority, the municipal authorities and the administration of municipal affairs would automatically be Turkish.

The objection can be raised that, in view of historical precedents, constitutional guarantees of minority rights are not enough is such guarantees are always at the mercy of the majority. Such rights have always been the following:

(a) To enjoy their own culture;
(b) To use their own language;
(c) To establish their own schools;
(d) To profess and pactise their own religion;
(e) To enjoy full autonomy in matters of personal status, such as marriage and dicorce;
(f) To have their own educational, cultural and social organizations;
(g) To issue newspapers in their own language.[5] To these, in the case of Cyprus, must also be added:

1 The right to participate in Government and all other organs of State;
2 To form part of the personnel of the military and civil services of the state and of the judiciary;
3 To be freely admitted to all professions on the basis of ability alone and complete freedom of economic enterprise and employment without any discrimination on the grounds of race, religion or number.

To ensure these rights to a minority over and above the normal constitutional guarantees it might be useful for the Republic of Cyprus to enter into a number of treaties and agreements with the U.N. whereby a U.N. Commissioner with the task of supervising human rights would be permanently in residence in Cyprus and be answerable only to the Secretary-General. The treaties will ensure that U.N. intervention will not have to be authorized by the Republic of Cyprus in order to be effective.[6]

Finally, there is the question of guarantees for the Republic of Cyprus as a whole. The Zurich-London agreements have failed to work because the three guarantors not only had interests in Cyprus but conflicting interests.[7] In particular, the choice of Greece and Turkey was an unfortunate one because it was like assigning foxes to guarantee the safety of chickens! The new guarantors should exclude Greece and Turkey, if not Britain as well. The guarantors should also act outside the U.N. in order to avoid the Security Council veto. In other words, the guarantors should be a group of powers subscribing to the treaty among themselves and countersigned by the Republic of Cyprus to defend, by military means if necessary, the independence and integrity of the Republic of Cyprus upon appeal by the legal government of the island. Such a treaty would be similar to the treaties setting up and guaranteeing the independence and neutrality of Belgium in the 19th Century.

In addition Greece and Turkey might conclude a treaty with each other agreeing not to instigate or tolerate any change in the status of the Republic of Cyprus as well as giving up the use of armed forces while acting on their own in order to maintain or alter the status of the Republic of Cyprus. In other words, Greece and Turkey under such a treaty could only act in unison in respect of Cyprus. Such a treaty would not constitute a treaty of guarantee for Cyprus but only an agreement between Greece and Turkey to act amicably over any problems involving Cyprus.

The above suggestions for a hopeful solution to the Cyprus problem are based on the sentiment that the basic idea of the 1960 settlement that Cyprus should be a unitary state was correct. What was principally wrong with this settlement was the divided and impotent structure of the central Government envisaged by the Constitution as well as ill-defined provisions concerning the separate Turkish municipalities (Turkish majority areas). Another glaring fault, the removal of which might bring harmony, was the nature of the guarantor powers, all either interested or uninterested in Cyprus. The lack of effective extra-constitutional guarantees for the Turkish community encouraged a spirit of impasse and suspicion. But above all the Greek Cypriot commitment to enosis with disregard to the effect it had on the Turkish community and the Turkish desire for partition and federation, which meant the displacement of the Greek element, were the major gravediggers of the 1960 settlement. If both sides were to lay aside these concepts and genuinely get down to functional co-operation within the organs of the state created, they would find in time that, like many married couples, they could live very well together in one household without passionately loving each other. It is such commitment to political structures and not love that creates viable states and ensures a future for their citizens. It is only to be hoped that this truth will be realized in Cyprus and by all those friends of Cyprus who wish for and can be responsible for a just and speedy solution of its problems.

IX
Analysis of the most recent event

The most significant event in Cyprus since the Turkish invasion has been the return on 7th December 1974 of Archbishop Makarios as the legitimate President. His return had not been favoured[1] by the United States and Britain on the grounds that he was not popular with the Turks. This was rather contradictory as Turkey allegedly invaded Cyprus in order to restore the Archbishop's Government and to restore the status quo after the coup of 15th July 1974. Nevertheless, the return of the Archbishop led to another change of face by the Turks as well as by all the others who opposed his return. Turkish suspicions of Makarios remain, but whereas the Turkish Cypriot leadership declared before his return that they would not negotiate with him, they said only a few days later that his return provided 'positive aspects'.[2] The return of the Archbishop has been linked to the beginning of energetic reconstruction in the Greek areas of Cyprus, partly to repair the damage caused by military action and partly to produce expanded economic activity in order to secure employment for the refugees whom the Archbishop considers to be his first care and responsibility.

An even more important aspect of the return of Archbishop Makarios, and perhaps one of the most 'positive aspects' referred to by the Turkish Cypriot leadership was the resumption of the intercommunal talks on 14th January 1975, between Glafcos Clerides and Raouf Denktash. These talks were suspended on 13th February 1975 when Mr. R. Denktash promoted himself to the Head[3] of the 'Federated Turkish Cypriot State'. The Government of Archbishop Makarios appealed to the Security Council against such an illegal and unilateral action. It is interesting to note here that this declaration came as Turkey considered written proposals from President Makarios for a settlement based on cantons and a federal system of government.[4]

After several days of deliberation a Resolution was unanimously adopted by the Security Council on 12th March 1975[5] calling on the two sides to resume their intercommunal talks under Dr. Kurt Waldheim's 'personal auspices'.[6]

Both sides agreed to take part in the renewal of the talks held in Vienna on 28th April 1975[7], which, however, served no useful purpose because of the unreasonable Turkish demand on a 50:50 across the board participation in all aspects of Cypriot political life and economy. When the talks were resumed in Vienna between the 5th and the 7th of June, they were adjourned till the 24th-27th of July when the Greek Cypriots agreed to the transfer of approximately 9,000 Turks from the Greek zone to the Turkish zone of Cyprus on the understanding that 10,000 Greek Cypriots in the Turkish zone would be allowed to stay there. The talks were again adjourned, this time to New York to be held on 8th September. At this round of talks, however, nothing was achieved because Mr. Denktash did not come forward with any new constitutional proposals but produced a virtual ultimatum that a partition of Cyprus must be recognized before he would be willing to discuss with his Greek partners any proposals as to the structure of the government of the Bi-zonal Federal State.

This induced the government of Archbishop Makarios to bring the Cyprus issue once more before the United Nations for its agenda. On November 20th the General Assembly of the United Nations voted 117 for and 1 against (Turkey) on a resolution put forward by five non-aligned nations (India, Yugoslavia, Algeria, Guyana and Mali) demanding the withdrawal of all foreign troops from the island and the return of all refugees to their homes, and the immediate resumption of the Greek-Turkish intercommunal talks under the chairmanship of the Secretary-General of the United Nations who was required to report on the progress of the negotiations by March 1976.

Since the writing of the previous chapter, and before

publication, certain events have occurred in the Cyprus situation which it would be interesting to analyze with reference to the proposals outlined in that chapter. The events in question have been the breakdown of the current intercommunal talks and the resignation of Glafcos Clerides; the publication of the two Cypriot communities proposals; the evidence of the systematic expulsion of the Greek Cypriots from the Turkish occupied zone and their replacement by Turkish colonists[8] from the mainland in an attempt to permanently alter the demographic character of Cyprus; and the April 1976 Report from the House of Commons Select Committee on Cyprus, which was highly critical of Britain's role in the Turkish invasion of Cyprus.

The universally held view has been that the future of Cyprus depended on the talks between the two communities which have become an institution since 1964. Between 1964-1974 Raouf Denktash and Glafcos Clerides had held two hundred[9] meetings without producing any results. After the events of 1974 no one could think of a better idea to resolve the crisis than to reinstate the intercommunal talks with the same protagonists, but this time under the chairmanship of Dr. Waldheim, U.N. Secretary-General. During this latest round Clerides and Denktash met five times. These meetings ended with the publication of the proposals of both sides and subsequent resignation of Glafcos Clerides, following the complete failure to reach any understanding. Until the end of 1975 the Turkish side managed not to produce any proposals by using various pretexes. Only on February 17th, 1976, at a meeting in Vienna, Denktash and Clerides reached a secret agreement whereby the Greek Cypriots were to produce fresh proposals by March 23rd, which were to be countered with Turkish Cypriot proposals within a period of ten days.[10] The Turkish Cypriots found the Greek Cypriot proposals unacceptable and rejected and published them without producing any proposals of their own. Clerides had made a major mistake by revealing to the Turks the ultimate Greek proposals while allowing them to hold back their own. This trick discredited Clerides who resigned on April 9th, 1976 and was replaced by Tassos Papodopoulos. After this resignation on 17th April the

Turkish Cypriots published their proposals for the solution of the Cyprus problem.

The essence of the Turkish proposals can be summed up as 'partition and blackmail'. The Turkish plan falls into two parts. The first part lays down the principles concerning the establishment of a federal state in Cyprus consisting of two separate communal states. The second part deals with the powers of the proposed central federal government. The element constituting partition linked with blackmail is contained in points 1 and 14 of the General Principles. Point 1 reads:

'Cyprus should be a federal Republic comprised of two federated states, one in the north for the Turkish national community and one in the south for the Greek national community'.

This proposal clearly aims at the establishment of two separate states in Cyprus on clear geographical and racial lines. It can only be described as partition pure and simple, and the end of Cyprus as one viable Sovereign state.[11] If the Greek Cypriots were to accept this principle as the basis for negotiations, they could hope for concessions from the Turkish side for the refugees driven out from their houses in the Turkish zone, and this is clearly contained in point 14 of the General Principles which runs as follows:

'The question of proprietary rights and claims arising therefrom or relating thereto, as well as any other claims, shall be settled by mutual agreement between the parties concerned, in conjunction with the question of compensation and other related matter, in such a manner as not to obstruct the setting up of the proposed Federal Republic'.

In addition the Turkish side offered certain unspecified territorial concessions to the Greeks if they were to accept the bi-zonal partition as a framework for negotiations. On the basis of such territorial concessions in favour of the Greeks, Glafcos Clerides accepted the proposals. But Makarios made known his dissatisfaction with any negotiations on the basis of a permanent partition of Cyprus.

It has become evident that, in the light of his experience, President Makarios has decided that no agreement for the present would be better than an unsatisfactory agreement. Unlike his acceptance of the unsatisfactory Constitution of 1960, there is now no Greek Government exercising pressure on him to accept partition. Accordingly, he prefers to accept the challenge of a moral issue with the support of almost all the Greek Cypriots. President Makarios and the Greek Cypriots are prepared to pay the price of rejecting partition—a smaller territory for the Greek community in Cyprus and lack of compensation for the uprooted and looted Greek population from the north. In addition, the rejection of[12] the Turkish proposals may mean the unhindered colonization by mainland Turks of the Turkish occupied zone of Cyprus.

The second part of the Turkish proposals, originally proposed in July 1975, concern the proposed federal government. Only very few and very vague powers are to be vested in this type of federal government. These powers include foreign affairs with a 50:50 participation of both communities in the personnel; External Defence; Federal Courts; Federal Budget; and various other minor services. In defence matters no federal forces are intended but both federated states are to maintain their own forces on their own territory at the disposal of the federated government. The federal budget is to be made dependent on the budgets to be maintained by the two federated states. The federal communications and telecommunication services are to co-exist with similar services maintained by each of the federated states with what the Proposals call 'its respective mother country.' Really, under the Turkish Proposals the envisaged federal Government is only a status symbol without any powers or clearly defined duties and responsibilities. The establishment of such an order would make the two respective federated states virtually independent of each other and dependent on Greece and Turkey.

The Greek Cypriot Proposals, as mentioned already, were handed to Raouf Denktash on March 24th, 1976, and revealed by him prematurely thus betraying the confidence placed in him by his fellow negotiator Glafcos Clerides. These Proposals bear a strong resemblance to the settlement of the Cyprus problem advocated in Chapter VIII of this book. In short, the Proposals point to a return to the 1960 position but without the disadvantages and prejudices embodied in the Constitution of that year. The main points are the desire to maintain Cyprus as a unitary state and a strong central Government which will control foreign affairs, defence, finance, telecommunications, ports and airports. The powers and duties of the federal Government are divided among 26 headings in the Proposals. Furthermore, the Greek Cypriots insist that on the federal level the two communities must be represented proportionately to their numerical ratios that is 82 percent Greek and 18 percent Turkish. On the other hand the Greek Cypriot Proposals do not object to the establishment of two separate Greek and Turkish regions though not necessarily along the boundary line established by the Turkish occupation force but consisting of no less that 20 percent of the territory of the Republic. The two Regions would enjoy extensive powers of local Government, coming under 24 headings in the Proposals. In other words, the Greek side concedes the long standing Turkish demand that the Turks should live separately and administer their own area. At the same time the Greek Cypriots stress that the economic unity of the Republic should be maintained and strengthened; all citizens of the Republic should enjoy the right of free movement throughout the territory of the Republic, and the right to work and reside in any place of his choice which would mean the return of all the refugees, Greek and Turkish, to their original places of residence. Above all the Greeks demanded the withdrawal of all foreign military forces from Cyprus—a point not raised for obvious reasons in the Turkish Proposals of 17th April 1976.

The two sets of Proposals are in stark opposition to each other on two most important points. The first one is the continuous Turkish military occupation of the present Turkish zone of Cyprus and the expulsion of the Greek population from that area. The Turkish Proposals completely ignore this aspect of the situation.[13] The second point is the obvious fact that the Turkish Cypriots want the establishment of two separate states, one in the north for the Turkish national community and one in the south for the Greek national community. In practice, under the Turkish Proposals there would be no link between these two states. In other words, the

Turks use Bi-zonalism to mean partition.

Concerning the Greek Cypriot refugees, it is interesting to note that, while the Turkish Proposals do not even mention them, they do in the explanatory note to the Proposals draw attention to the fact that between 1955 and 1973 the Turkish population had been driven out by the Greeks from their homes. This is a clear reference to the Turkish enclaves which existed from 1963-1974. But the fact remains that the Turkish population chose to go into these enclaves of their own accord and that they were free to leave them (and in fact some of them did leave them) at any time. At no point were the Turks of Cyprus driven out of their homes and deprived of their property by foreigners except for a few isolated incidents in 1963-64. The Cyprus Government hastened to condemn such acts and constantly invited all Turks to return to their homes under the protection of the U.N. Peace-Keeping forces.[14]

In the meantime, startling events have taken place in the economic life of Cyprus. In less than two years since the Turkish invasion and despite the crowding into Greek Cyprus of 200,000 refugees expelled by the Turkish army, the economy of Greek Cyprus has been booming.[15] A full account of this miraculous recovery is summarized in detail by the Economist Intelligence Unit, Quarterly Economic Review No. 2-1976.

Perhaps the most serious development in the Cyprus problem is the determination of President Makarios to engage in a long struggle with his Turkish adversaries. This means that, whatever may come, Makarios is determined to sit it out. The price which Greek Cyprus is paying for such a policy has already been touched upon. But there is an even greater danger. Constant reports from the Turkish occupied area of Cyprus mention the arrival in Turkish controlled Cyprus of colonists from mainland Turkey. Turkey is in a position to alter the demographic status of Cyprus by a policy of colonization[16] to reinforce the Turkish claim to 40 percent of the island. The longer it takes to reach a settlement the more likelihood of the Turkish plans succeeding. Unfortunately, further evidence has come to light[17] that the Turkish army in Cyprus, after having driven out the original Greek inhabitants has now been engaging in the destruction of Greek churches and cemeteries in order to remove all evidence of previous Greek occupancy of the area from which they have been driven out. One is reminded of a similar policy pursued by Turkey in her Armenian provinces where the same course of events took place. Such imperialism bodes ill for any possible future co-existence in Cyprus between the two communities. 'The vandalism and desecration are so methodical and so widespread that they amount to institutionalized obliterations of everything sacred to a Greek. Overtly or covertly the process must have been perceived and approved by an administration that only a fortnight ago was mobilising international Moslem opinion to protest over the burning down of a mosque that is in fact still standing intact—we filmed it.'[18] One wonders, when contemplating such savagery, what would have been the attitude of Kemal Ataturk when confronted with this handiwork of his successors.

From what has been said the situation of Turkey has not been improved by her adventure in Cyprus. Turkey has lost many friends. The Aegean oil dispute with Greece is not going to be made any easier by the Turkish conduct in Cyprus. Except for the contradictory U.S. policy towards Turkey there is a growing isolation of that country within N.A.T.O. Furthermore, the cost to Turkey of maintaining 40,000 troops in Cyprus is not exactly an economic blessing, and Turkish occupied Cyprus is not economically viable enough to maintain itself, let alone an army of occupation. Turkey is facing both internal and external difficulties which manifest themselves in constant governmental instability. Perhaps, in the near future, Turkey will have to pay the full price for having been the main agent in the destruction of N.A.T.O. in the eastern Mediterranean. Anyhow, the onus for the rejection of any just and equitable solution of the Cyprus problem must rest fairly and squarely on Turkey and not on the Turkish Cypriot community which has been as much the victim of Turkish military imperialism and adventurism as the Greek Cypriots.

The final comment on the events in Cyprus is concerned with Britain's failure to act under the Treaty of Guarantee as expressed in the Report[19] from the Select Committee on

Cyprus ordered by the House of Commons to be printed in April 1976. The Report consists of sixty-eight pages of minutes of its hearings and eighteen appendices. The gist of the Report[20] is that Britain acted both illegally and immorally by not preventing the Turkish invasion of Cyprus of 1974. The Select Committee puts the blame squarely on the then British Foreign Secretary, James Callaghan. 'Britain had a legal right, a moral obligation, and the military capacity to intervene in Cyprus during July and August 1974. She did not intervene for reasons which the Government refuses to give.'[21] It is to be noted that Callaghan defended himself from these charges by claiming credit for arranging the ceasefire in Cyprus and the Foreign Office went into action and rejected the Report of the Committee as not being impartial and constructive. The Sunday Times of May 23rd, 1976, interpreted British policy at that time by an assumption that the British Government did not know nor believe that Turkey was going to invade Cyprus. The article in question quotes that the Turkish Prime Minister at that time, Mr. B. Ecevit, during his visit to London to consult with the British Government about any possible action under the Treaty of Guarantee in respect of the coup in Cyprus, gave Callaghan his personal guarantee that Turkey would not invade.[22] One is reminded of the personal assurance. both in word and in writing, supplied by Hitler to Neville Chamberlain in Munich in 1938 to the effect that Germany would not violate the sovereignty of Czechoslovakia nor resort to war in furtherance of any of its claims. It is to be regretted that, with the memories of Munich still alive, British statesmen can be still influenced by a 'personal guarantee' given by foreign statesmen who are determined ultimately to apply *ultima ratio regis*.

X
Conclusion – Prospects

It appears that the Turkish leadership used to think Archbishop Makarios largely responsible for the intercommunal problem. The Turkish Cypriots have always expressed a dislike for the Archbishop. They cannot help disliking him because as a priest he is a symbolic expression of hostile Greek Nationalism and thus the standard bearer of the idea of enosis. They also cannot help associating him with the events of the 1950's and the beginning of their troubles. Their attitude can be summed up by the belief that had it not been for Makarios everything would have been alright and in order under the continued British rule of Cyprus. Makarios is indispensable; they dislike him but they need him. This attitude is curiously reflected by some of the Greek opponents of the Archbishop. They resent Makarios for having deviated from the right wing policy of enosis, but they equally feel lost without him and, with Grivas dead, they have no alternative personality to rally around.

After the events of December 1963, the Greek Cypriots believed that time was on their side but, as events turned out, this proved not to be the case. Today it is reported that the Turks, fortified by the presence of the Turkish army, also feel that time is on their side. They may be as wrong in this as the Greek Cypriots had been. The history of Cyprus seems to show that time is on nobody's side but, on the contrary, seems to be working against everybody. The sooner this is realized by the parties concerned, the better they would be placed to find their way to a truly realistic and pragmatic solution to their problems. Certainly the time has come for a positive response to the sighs of the Cypriots. Their future should be guaranteed and out of the present chaos, drama and pathos of Cyprus there should now come forward a brave and just answer putting an end to the agony of its people who have, undoubtedly, been the victims of a major international scandal.

There are also the wider international implications of the Cyprus problem. The events in Cyprus in 1974 have led to the fall of the military regime in Greece and the restoration of a parliamentary Government under the aegis of the veteran statesman, Constantine Karamanlis, who spent the entire period of the dictatorship in exile. It has already been stressed that the military regime had reduced Greece to a calamitous political, economic and military position. Greece, at present, has not got the sufficient power and therefore, determination, to confront Turkey, least of all in Cyprus itself where geography is against her. For this reason, there has been no major eruption between Greece and Turkey. However, if the cause of hellenism is brutally suppressed in Cyprus, a government might well emerge in Greece which will attempt to vindicate the situation if need be arms in hand. Greece is in a better position than Turkey to adopt a policy on non-alignment as she is not a border country with Soviet Russia as Turkey is. Such a policy of non-alignment will produce for Greece an adequate supply of modern armaments to confront Turkey which at present is in a more advantageous position. A conflict in the Aegean between Greece and Turkey will irreparably damage N.A.T.O. of which Turkey is an indispensable member. Therefore, it is against the true interests of the N.A.T.O. powers including Turkey itself to allow such a state of affairs to develop. The powers of the world, particularly the Western Powers, must realize this and draw together to impose a solution of the Cyprus problem entailing the independence, integrity and neutrality of the island in case of any possible opposition on the part of Turkey. The 19th Century showed that solutions imposed by powers acting in concert, although not always ideal, always produced lengthy periods of peace. The imposition of a solution by force or threat of force should only be carried out in the event of the Cyprus problem escalating into full scale warfare, perhaps leading to a major conflict.

The Cyprus problem must be viewed from the point of either a *solution* or a *settlement*. The difference between the two is that the former implies a radical change in the situation whereas the latter implies a regularization of the existing situation. In the case of Cyprus a solution would be the removal of the Turkish minority to Turkey with full compensation and resettlement funds guaranteed by international agreements. Such course of action would be a continuation of the Ataturk-Venizelos treaty of 1923 dealing with the exchange of populations. Naturally, the entirely ethnically Greek state of Cyprus, after the departure of the Turkish community, would have to agree to the exclusion of enosis from its future policy. On the other hand, with enosis also excluded, a settlement of the Cyprus problem should not entail any transfers of populations but should endeavour to re-establish in every sense the state of affairs in Cyprus which existed in 1960. In this case the constitution of 1960 should be made to work by effectively streamlining it, and the sovereignty of the Cypriot state and its constitution should be guaranteed, in addition to Greece and Turkey, by the two super-powers i.e. the U.SA. and the U.S.S.R. Maybe the question of guarantees is more important in view of the events of the past twenty years than any constitutional niceties. Both the communities in Cyprus would be unable to have any confidence in the future without cast iron guarantees of armed forces being available against any possible violator of the status quo.

Next, this last observation should be made concerning the conflict between the two communities in Cyprus. Not too much stress should be put on drafting an ideal Constitution for the state. Rather a line of political agreement should be encouraged to emerge leaving the exact constitutional niceties aside. History has proved that the most perfect Constitutions have failed to work if there was no political agreement to operate them. Conversely, the most ramshackled Constitutions or even the lack of any Constitution (as in the case of Britain) have proved successful if a political atmosphere exists to make the institutions of the state work. The moral here is to establish a kind of political co-operation and then the constitutional aspects will develop themselves. It is to be hoped that this might be the case with Cyprus.

At this point in time certain realities have emerged from the situation which must be taken fully into consideration when a solution or even a settlement is proposed. The most prominent feature is that, with the aid of the Turkish army the Cypriot Turks have created their own state of Cyprus on a firm territorial basis. The Cypriot Turks, therefore, will only negotiate with the Greek Cypriots on the basis of the existence and entrenchment of such a state. The Greek Cypriot side, on the other hand, can never accept such a state of affairs, especially when created by force. Accordingly, the intercommunal talks between the two sides have now become a complete farce because the two sides are definitely on different planes—the Greek Cypriots thinking in terms of a united Cypriot State and the Turkish Cypriot of two separate states in Cyprus. It is rather a sanguine belief that the intercommunal talks after 1974 could achieve something which they could not in the ten years between 1964-1974.

The de facto existence of two states in Cyprus brings into focus two possible developments. The first is the effectual partition of Cyprus between Greece and Turkey, the so-called 'double enosis'. But such a solution seems likely to be avoided by both Greece and Turkey because it would give them a common frontier running across a conflict-torn island, and would make such a frontier, with Greek and Turkish troops confronting each other, highly vulnerable and inflammable. The second development, which might also cause an armed conflict between Greece and Turkey, would be a Turkish occupation of the entire island of Cyprus. This eventuality, however, would undoubtedly trigger off a major terrorist-guerrilla response from the Greek population. This, in turn, would constitute an unbearable pressure on the Greek Government to seek a military solution which might result in a war between the two countries and the collapse of N.A.T.O. in the Mediterranean.

The danger of a major war is now closely associated with the Cyprus problem. The United Nations are paralysed by disunity among the Security Council powers. A more hopeful contingency would be action by the major powers outside the

U.N. A Conference of powers should appoint, on lines suggested by Lord Caradon,[1] a negotiating committee composed of representatives of the N.A.T.O. and Warsaw Pact powers plus a representative of the non-aligned powers. The Committee should move between Cyprus, Athens and Ankara, and, on the lines practised by Dr. Henry Kissinger, excercise the maximum pressure to bring all parties to the dispute to some common denominator for a settlement. Needless to say, the Conference of the powers would be pledged to enforce a solution which would be fair and just to both the communities and least likely to endanger peace. Such a solution, in order to be viable, would have to respect the organic unity of the island as well as all the rights of the different components of its population. Separation and partition by force and intimidation should not be on the agenda. Only the cohabitation of all the inhabitants of Cyprus within one structure can spell out any hope for the island. All those who desire peace in Cyprus and peace in the world should bear this constantly in mind.

Those who contemplate the problem of Cyprus in 1977 realize that they are standing at a cross-roads. One road leads to the establishment of two separate states on the island and perpetual conflict, and the other leads to a compromise settlement in which there will be neither dispossession nor oppression as Cyprus will remain unified but the Turkish minority will be given all that they demanded under the Constitution of 1960 and even more. In exchange for relinquishing the veto they would acquire the right to hold the presidency. The future course of events in Cyprus can only follow either of these two roads, and all future developments will have to conform to this pattern. Turkish oppression of the Greeks has constituted the history of the two peoples since the Turkish conquest of the Byzantine world. After more than a quarter of a century of unfinished agony any other alternatives have been exhausted. Let it be hoped that, whatever happens, the people of Cyprus, will ultimately survive whatever ordeal is reserved for them, as they have always survived in the past. They will suffer and wait and struggle until they obtain what all human beings are entitled to—justice and freedom.

It is felt that only if the two communities in Cyprus will

cease offending and provoking each other will there be the possiblity of creating the appropriate atmosphere for the grounding of common Cypriot citizenship, entirely grounded independent of both Greece and Turkey, and in which both communities will have an equal vested interest despite their wide ethnic and cultural differences. The creation of a Cypriot nationhood is *ipso facto* ruled out.[2] Also, unfortunately, it is not always remembered that such a thing as the modern concept of citizenship has never existed in Cyprus; it must be created now. This concept of common citizenship must replace the relationship between the conquerors and the conquered which, in one sense or another from 1571 to the present day, has in fact ruled the relationship between Greeks and Turks in Cyprus. Only if those who are responsible for the shaping of vital decisions face this fact and recognize it for what it is can there be any real hope for a bloodless and lasting settlement of the problem which has brought darkness and despair to the beautiful island of Cyprus. It is time for the agony of Cyprus to end. The curtain should come down on a scene which has been bespattered with blood for years. It is hard to understand that playing the waiting game can bring any lasting advantages to anyone concerned. The misery and horror inflicted on both the communities in Cyprus can only have a terrible outcome in the future if reason and humanity do not prevail and the problem is not tackled immediately with realism and imagination. True and meaningful negotiations should replace procrastination which, since 1974 has served as the basis for the so-called negotiations. Any attempt to alter the character of Cyprus by force will inevitably cause a catastrophe, the results of which will be felt far beyond the confines of Cyprus, Greece and Turkey.

Notes

Introduction
1 See: The *Times*, 15.2.75 and 8th Sept. 75. Also: Report from the Select Committee on Cyprus, H.M.S.O., session 1975-76, 8th Apr. 1976.

Chapter 1
1 The size of Cyprus is 3,572 square miles and its total population is about 632,000 people.
2 Cyprus, through its long history, was subjected to many conquerors: Assyrians, Egyptians, Persians, Romans, Franks, Turks and British.
3 By the Treaty of Defensive Alliance between Greece, Britain and Turkey of 1878, the latter assigned the island to be occupied and administered by Britain. On 5th November 1914, Britain annexed Cyprus, and Turkey recognised this fact in Article 20 of the Treaty of Lausanne, 1923.
4 Turkey, by Article 16 of the Treaty of Lausanne, has renounced any right or title over Cyprus and by Article 27 of the same Treaty, divested itself of the exercise of any power or jurisdiction in political, legislative, or administrative matters over the nationals of Cyprus.
5 E.O.K.A.: National Organisation of Cypriot Fighters.
6 'These Agreements, however, have not been the result of the full expression of the will of the people of Cyprus. They were imposed upon them from outside. In the prevailing circumstances at the time there was no choice. Rejection of the Agreement would have meant denial of the independence and increased bloodshed.'
From a speech made by Archbishop Makarios at the Conference of Non-Aligned Countries at Cairo on 9th October 1964. See: *Cyprus Today*, 1964, p. 6.
7 Cyprus: Reluctant Republic, Mouton, The Hague, Paris, 1973.
8 For the Archbishop's reaction, see: (a) S. G. Xydis, op. cit. p.p. 422-460; (b) Robert Stephens: *Cyprus: A Place of Arms*, Pall Mall, 1966, p.p. 163-167; (c) H. D. Purcell, *Cyprus*, Ernest Benn Lts., 1969; (d) J. A. Stegenga: *The United Nations Force in Cyprus*, Ohio State Univ. Press, 1968, p. 23; (e) L. Ierodiakonou: *The Cyprus Question*, Stockholm 1971, p.p. 219-221; (f) D. Alastos: *Cyprus Guerrilla*, Heinemann, 1960, p.p.

198-200; (g) P. N. Vanezis: *Makarios: Pragmatism v. Idealism*, Abelard Schuman, London, 1974, p.p. 103-4; (h) *Critical Hours* (in Greek) D. Bitsios, Athens, 1973, p.p. 120-122; (i) *Makarios and His Allies* (in Greek) A. E. Xydis, Athens, 1972, p.p. 328-337.

9 'The Bishop of Kition and the Abbot of Kykko, who were present, absolutely agreed with what Britain and Vlachos had said. They appealed to Makarios to go ahead with the agreement that would bring independence to Cyprus . . .'
Xydis, op. cit. p. 422.

10 *Cyprus*, H.M.S.O., Cmnd. 1093, 1960.

11 *The Economist*, 20-26 July, 1974, p. 61: 'The 1960 settlement produced a Frankenstein monster of a constitution which was patently unfair to the Greeks.'

12 H.M.S.O., op. cit. p. 91.

13 (a) See Ierodiakonou, op. cit. p.p. 232-34; (b) S. Kyriskides: *Cyprus Constitutionalism and Crisis Government*, Philadelphia 1968. The regime established in Cyprus was according to Tsirimokos a 'monstrosity'.—Xydis, op. cit. p. 462.

14 For a full analysis of the Constitution, see: (a) *Cyprus, The Problem in Perspective*, P.I.O., Nicosia, 1969; (b) *Cyprus in Search of a Constitution*, P. Polyviou, Cyprus, 1976.

15 Xydis, op. cit. p. 462.

16 The House of Representatives would consist of 35 Greek and 15 Turkish Members.

17 The Greek Communal Chamber ceased to function and by the transfer of the competences of the Greek Communal Chamber and the Ministry of Education Law, 1965, all its competences were transferred to the newly created Ministry of Education and other organs of the State as in the Law provided.
See: *Constitutional and Legal Problems in the Republic of Cyprus*, P.I.O., Nicosia, 1968, p. 14.

18 *The Problem in Perspective*, Nicosia, 1969, p. 13.

19 *Le Monde*, Paris, February 7th, 1964.
'The Turkish minority of Cyprus was given rights and privileges that it never enjoyed before, not even under the Ottoman occupation.'

20 Xydis, op. cit., p.p. 461-462.

21 In 1882, the British Government granted a Constitution to Cyprus providing for a Legislative Council composed of six official members and twelve elected members. Of the elected members, nine were Greek and three Turks. The British High Commissioner, as he was called then, enjoyed the casting vote. After the uprising of 1931, the Legislative Council was dissolved and Britain went ahead with the eliminating of constitutional rule and the establishment of a rather authoritarian regime.

22 P. G. Polyviou: *Cyprus: The Tragedy and the Challenge*, printed by John Swain & Sons Ltd., London, 1975, p. 28.

23 Xydis, op. cit. p. 439.

Chapter II
1 By this I mean that Archbishop Makarios was fully conscious of the future difficulties.
2 A.K.E.L. = Progressive Party of the Working People.
3 Archbishop Makarios received 144,501 votes against 71,753 votes for John Clerides, Q.C., father of Mr. Glafcos Clerides, President of the House of Representatives.
4 P. N. Vanezis, op. cit. p. 112.
5 See: (a) R. Stephens, op. cit. p. 175; (b) L. Ierodiakonou, op. cit. p. 237.
6 H. D. Purcell, p. cit. p. 303.
7 R. Stephens, op. cit. p. 175.
8 Ierodiakonou, op. cit. p. 236; Vanezis, op. cit. p. 116.
9 See: (a) Ierodiakonou, op. cit. p. 237; (b) Vanezis, op. cit. p. 116.
10 Purcell, op. cit. p. 314.
11 See: (a) Stephens op. cit. p. 163; (b) Purcell, op. cit. p. 313; (c) Venezis, op. cit. p. 116.
12 See: Stephens, op. cit. p. 173.
13 See: (a) Stephens, op. cit. p. 176; (b) Vanezis, op. cit. p. 117; (c) Ierodiakonou, op. cit. p.p. 238-9.
14 See: (a) Vanezis, op. cit. p. 117; (b) Stephens, op. cit. p.p. 176-7; (c) Purcell, op. cit. p. 316.
15 Xydis, op. cit. p. 485.
16 Stegenga, p. 30.
17 It is generally believed that Makarios was encouraged to submit his proposals by the then British High Commissioner, Sir Arthur Clarke.
18 See: (a) Stephens, op. cit. p.p. 179-80; (b) Purcell, op. cit. p. 321; (c) Ierodiakonou, op. cit. p. 251; (d) Harbottle, op. cit. p. 10; (e) Stegenga, op. cit. p. 30.
19 Harbottle, op. cit. p.p. 12-14.
20 Purcell, op. cit. p.p. 332-333; Vanezis, op. cit. p. 126; Stegenga, op. cit. p.p. 35-36; Ierodiakonou, op. cit. p.p. 258-259.

Chapter III
1 T.M.T. = Turk Mudafaa Teskilati = Turkish Defence Organisation.
2 On October 18th 1959, a British minesweeper intercepted the Turkish motor-boat Deniz, smuggling ammunition into Cyprus: Ierodiakonou, op. cit. p. 242.
3 Purcell, op. cit. p. 319.
4 Harbottle, op. cit. p. 12; Stephens, op. cit. p.p. 182-4.
5 Purcell, op. cit. p. 332.
6 Harbottle, op. cit. p. 14; See also Stegenga, op. cit. p. 36.
7 Ierodiakonou, op. cit. p. 259.
8 Harbottle, op. cit. p. 43.
9 In June, 1964, Grivas left Athens and arrived in Cyprus and was appointed Commander of the National Guard.
10 Purcell, op. cit. p. 348; Ierodiakonou, op. cit. p. 260.

11 Harbottle, op. cit. p.p. 53-54.
12 Stegenga, op. cit. p.p. 46-47.
13 *Economist*, March 14th, 1964, p. 979.
14 Stegenga, op. cit. p. 40.
15 Stegenga, op. cit. p.p. 39-40.
16 Stephens, op. cit. p. 185.
17 Purcell, op. cit. p. 355.
18 Purcell, op. cit. p. 342.
19 Purcell, op. cit. p. 359.
20 Purcell, op. cit. p. 360; ibid p. 361.
21 Purcell, op. cit. p. 361.
22 Purcell, op. cit. p. 362.
23 Purcell, op. cit. p. 362.
24 Taken from R. Stephens, op. cit. p.p. 202-203. For further reading on Plaza's Report, see: (i) Harbottle, op. cit. p.p. 55-56; (ii) Stegenga, op. cit. p.p. 9-, 135, 154; (iii) Stephens, op. cit. p.p. 202-203; (iv) Purcell, op. cit. p.p. 355-364; (v) Ierodiakonou, op. cit. p.p. 264-265; (vi) Vanezis, op. cit. p.p. 131-132; (vii) *Cyprus: The Problem in Perspective*, p.p. 25-26; (viii) P. G. Polyviou, op. cit. p. 42.
25 For further reading, see: (i) Ierodiakonou, op. cit. p.p. 262-63; (ii) D. Holden, *Greece Without Columns*, Faber & Faber, 1972, p. 209; (iii) Stephens, op. cit. p.p. 200-201; (iv) Vanezis, op. cit. p.p. 130-131; (v) A. Papandreou, *Democracy at Gunpoint*, A. Drutch, 1971, p.p. 104-105.
26 Panandreou, op. cit. p. 105.

Chapter IV
1 See: Jane Perry, Clark Carey and A. G. Carey, *The Web of Modern Greek Politics*, Columbia Univ. Press, 1968, p. 207.
2 Aspida (The Shield) was a group of Greek army officers serving in Cyprus, who under the 'leadership' of Andreas Papandreou, were to usurp power by violence, dethrone the King, turn Greece into a Soviet-style country and pull Greece out of N.A.T.O. The whole thing was framed-up. See: Holden, op. cit. p.p. 218-224.
3 Papandreou, op. cit. p. 224; Holden, op. cit. p. 219.
4 Papandreou, op. cit. p. 209.
5 For the detailed account of this battle, see: Harbottle, op. cit. p.p. 145-167.
6 Papandreou, op. cit. p. 210.
7 The London *Times* of 22nd November 1968 listed the following demands: (a) The recall of General Grivas; (b) The withdrawal of all Greek troops stationed in Cypus since 1964; (c) The disarmament of the Greek Cypriots; (d) The removal of pressure from the Turkish minority by ensuring freedom of movement; (e) Compensation for the victims and the damage caused to Turkish Cypriots at Agios Theodoras and Kophinou. See also: Ierodiakonou, op. cit. p. 270.
8 *Greece under Military Rule*, edited by R. Clogg & G. Yannopoulos Secker and Warburg, 1972, p. 203.

9 Makarios survived but on 15th March 1970 his Minister of the Interior and Defence, P. Georgadzis, was successfully liquidated because he knew too much about the plot against Makarios.
10 *Daily Telegraph*, 28 March 1972.
11 *Greece Under Military Rule*, p. 203.
12 *Cyprus: The Problem in Perspective*, Nicosia, 1969, p.p. 65-66.
13 Vanezis, op. cit. p.p. 184-185.
14 Vanezis, op. cit. p.p. 182-3.

Chapter V
1 *The Economist*, 20-26th July 1974, p. 59.
2 *Greece Under Military Rule*, p.p. 232-3.
3 Cyprus Bulletin, p. 10, 29th October 1974, p. 3.
4 Greece Under Military Rule, p.p. 236-237.
5 Vanezis, op. cit. p. 128.
6 Polyviou, op. cit. p. 49.
7 See Appendix I

Chapter VI
1 *The Economist*, 20-26th July 1974, p. 26.
2 *The Events in Cyprus*, Modinos, American Hellenic Institute, September 1974, p. 6.
3 *The Economist*, 20-26th July 1974, p. 11 and p. 26.
4 *News Week*, 29th July 1974, p.p. 11-12.
5 Grosvenor House Hotel, 26th November 1974.
6 It is of paramount historical importance to note that between 15th July and 20th July, not a single Turk was either killed or hurt in Cyprus.
7 *Cyprus Today*, Sept.-Oct. 1974, p.p. 7-10.
8 *New Statesman*, 23rd August 1974, p. 1.
9 See Appendix II.
10 See Appendix III.
11 Modinos, op. cit. p.p. 9-10; See also *Cyprus: Its Tragedy as a result of the Aggressive Invasion by Turkey*, p. 10, Nic. 1974.
12 Modinos, op. cit. p. 10.
13 Modinos, op. cit. p.p. 11-12.
14 *Cyprus Today*, Sept/Oct. 1974, 13-17.
15 See: *The Sun*, 5th Aug. 1974; *Daily Mail*, 10th Aug. 1974; *Daily Telegraph*, 22nd July 1974; *Liverpool Echo*, 31st Aug. 1974; *Reading Evening Post*, 24th Aug. 1974; *South Wales Argus*, 30th July 1974.
16 See: *Sunday Times*, 13th July 1975
17 *The Truth of the Turkish Invasion in Cyprus*, E.L.K.A., Athens, Greece, 1974, p. 6.
18 *Cyprus Bulletin*, 18th Oct. 1974, p. 3; *Cyprus: Its Tragedy as a result of the Aggressive Invasion by Turkey*, p.p. 23-26; *Cyprus Today*, August 1974, p.p. 36-37.
19 *Washington Post*, 4th Aug. 1974, Former Member of the White House Staff, dealing with the Mideast, 1961-66, and Ambassador to Turkey,

1968-69.

Chapter VII
1 *Economic Consequences of Turkish Invasion*, P.I.O., Oct. 1974, p. 1.
2 James Callaghan, then British Foreign and Commonwealth Relations Secretary, visited the Akrotiri Base, Limmasol, on 30th Dec. 1974, and on humanitarian grounds allowed the 8,000-10,000 Turkish Cypriot refugees to be airlifted to mainland Turkey and from there shipped back to the Turkish controlled Cyprus. (See *The Financial Times*, 22nd Jan. 1975; *The Times*, 22nd Jan. 1975; *The Daily Telegraph*, 23rd Jan. 1975.
3 *Daily Telegraph*, 29th Sept. 1975; *The Guardian*, 27th Nov. 1975.
4 Speech by Edward Kennedy, at a Dinner in aid of Cypriot Refugees at Waldorf Astoria Hotel in New York, on 19th October 1974.

Chapter VIII
1 See: P. N. Vanezis, London University M.A. Thesis, 1963. 'A Study of the Development of the Teaching of English in Cyprus with Special Reference to Political and Social Factors.'
2 *Constitutional Proposals for Cyprus*, H.M.S.O. 1956, p.p. 13-14.
3 See: *The Times*, 18th January 1975, Letter by Lord N. Bethell; Ibid, 15th March 1975, Letter by Patrick Leigh Fermor.
4 The President of the Republic, as Head of State, would be elected not by the electorate at large but by Parliament, as today under the West German, Italian and Indian Constitutions.
5 Polyviou, op. cit. p.p. 160-161.
6 See Chapter II.
7 See: *The Times*, 22nd March 1975, Leader; *The Spectator*, Aug. 24th, 1975, p. 232.

Chapter IX
1 *New Statesman*, 24th October 1975, Christopher Hitchens.
2 *The Sunday Times*, 15th December 1974.
3 *The Times*, 15th February 1975; *International Herald Tribune*, 14th February 1975; *Financial Times*, 14th February 1975; *The Guardian*, 14th March 1975.
4 See: *The Observer*, 9th February 1975.
5 See Appendix VII.
6 *International Herald Tribune*, 24th March 1975.
7 *The Guardian*, 4th April 1975. It was announced at the beginning that talks would take place on 21st April, then 25th, then 28th April.
8 The *Guardian*, 27th November 1975.
9 *Quarterly Economic Review*, No. 2, 1976, p. 15.
10 See: *The Times*, 15th April 1976.
11 *Note*: This Turkish stand has been predictable since Mr. Denktash had proclaimed his 'Turkish Federated State of Cyprus' with himself as President, on 13th February 1975.
12 *The Guardian*, 31st May 1976.

13 (Moreover, the Turkish side claims territory far in excess of the 20% offered to them by the Greek side on the basis of proportionality.)
14 See Chapter III.
15 *The Guardian*, 11th November 1976.
16 *The Financial Times*, 2nd November 1976; *The Guardian*, 27th November 1975.
17 *The Guardian*, 6th and 8th May 1976.
18 *The Guardian*, 6th May 1976.
19 Report from the Select Committee on Cyprus, H.M.S.O. April 1976.
20 See Comments in: (i) *The Times*, 20th May 1976; (ii) *The Guardian*, 20th May 1976; (iii) *The Evening Standard*, 20th May 1976; (iv) *The Daily Telegraph*, 20th May 1976.
21 *Select Committee Report*, p. xxi, see also *The Times*, 25th May 1976, p. 15.
22 *The Sunday Times*, 23rd May 1976.

Chapter X
1 *The Guardian*, 12th May 1976.
2 The ideas of nationhood is ruled out. What is intended is common citizenship binding the two communities in loyalty to the State, as in the case of the separate communities in Switzerland.

Bibliography

T. W. Adams, A.K.E.L.: *The Communist Party of Cyprus*, Hoover Institute Press, U.S.A., 1971.
T. W. Adams and A. V. Cottrell: *Cyprus between East and West*, John Hopkins Press, 1968.
D. Alastos: *Venizelos the Creator of Modern Greece*, London, 1942. *Cyprus in History*, Zeno Publishers, 1955. *Cyprus: Past and... Future*, London, 1943. *Cyprus Guerrilla*, Heinemann, 1960.
P. Arnold: *Cyprus Challenge*, Hogarth Press, 1956.
Sir S. Baker: *Cyprus as I saw it in 1879*, Macmillan, 1879.
P. Balfour: *The Orphaned Realm*, Percival Marshall, 1951.
D. Bavker: *Grivas: Portrait of a Terrorist*, Cresset, 1959.
D. Bitsios: *Cyprus: The Vulnerable Republic*, Institute for Balkan Studies, Thessaloniki, 1975.
S. Brown: *Three Months in Cyprus—During the Winter of 1878-9*, London 1879.
W. Byford-Jones: *Grivas and the Story of E.O.K.A.*, London, 1959.
S. Casson: *Ancient Cyprus*, Methuen, 1937.
R. Clogg and G. Yannopoulos: *Greece Under Military Rule*, Secker & Warbury, 1972.
C. A. Cobham: *Excerpta Cypria*, Cambridge University Press, 1908.
W. H. Dixon: *British Cyprus*, London, 1879.
Sir A. Eden: *Full Circle*, Cassell & Co., 1960.
F. H. Fisher: *Cyprus: Our New Colony*, Routledge, 1878.
Charles Foley: *Island in Revolt*, Longman, 1962. *Legacy of Strife, Cyprus from Rebellion to Civil War*, Penguin, 1964.
Sir H. Foot: *A Start in Freedom*, Hodder & Stoughton, 1964.
G. Grivas: *Memoirs*, Longman, 1964.

J. Hackett: *A History of the Orthodox Church of Cyprus*, Methuen, 1901.
M. Harbottle: *The Impartial Soldier*, O.U.P., 1970.
Sir G. Hill: *History of Cyprus* (4 vols.), Cambridge University Press, 1948-52.
D. Holden: *Greece without Columns*, Faber, 1972.
G. House: *Cyprus: Then and Now*, Dent, 1960.
L. Ierodiakonou: *The Cyprus Question*, Stockholm, 1971.
W. Kramidiotis: *The Cyprus Problem: The Proposed Solutions and the Concept of the Independent and Sovereign State*, Athens, 1975.
S. Kyriakides: *Cyprus: Constitutionalism and Crisis Government*, Philadelphia Press, 1968.
R. H. Long: *Cyprus: Its History, Its Present Resources and Future Prospects*, London, 1878.
D. E. Lee: *Great Britain and the Cyprus Question Policy of 1878*, Harvard University Press, 1934.
Sir H. Luke: *Cyprus under the Turks*, O.U.P., 1921. *Cyprus: An Appreciation*, Harrap, 1957.
H. Macmillan: *Riding the Storm*, Macmillan, 1971.
F. G. Maier: *Cyprus: From Earliest Times to the Present Day*, Elek, 1968.
S. Mayes: *Cyprus and Makarios*, Putnam, 1960.
A. V. Meyer & S. Vassiliou: *The Economy of Cyprus*, Harvard University Press, 1962.
P. Modinos: *The Events in Cyprus*, Paris, 1974, (in English).
C. W. J. Orr: *Cyprus Under British Rule*, Robert Scott, 1918.
A. Papandreou: *Democracy at Gunpoint*, Deutsch, 1971.
P. Polyviou: *The Tragedy and the Challenge*, John Swain & Son, London, 1975. *Cyprus in Search of a Constitution*, Nicosia, Cyprus, 1976.
H. D. Purcell: *Cyprus*, Benn, 1969.
J. A. Stegenga: *The United Nations Force in Cyprus*, Ohio State University Press, 1968.
R. Stephens: *Cyprus: A Place of Arms*, Pall Mall Press, 1966.
Sir R. Storrs: *Orientations*, Nicholson & Watson, 1937. *The Handbook of Cyprus*, Christophers, 1930.
C. G. Tornaritis: *Constitutional and Legal Problems in the Republic of Cyprus*, Nicosia, 1968. *The Turkish Invasion of*

Cyprus and Legal Problems arising therefrom, Nicosia, 1975.
Chr. A. Theodoulou: *The Cyprus Question: Some Facts*, Athens, 1975.
C. Tsoucalas: *The Greek Tragedy*, Penguin, 1969.
P. N. Vanezis: 'The Teaching of English in Cyprus with Special Reference to Social and Political Factors, 1878-1959', M.A. Thesis, London University, 1963. *Makarios: Faith and Power*, Abelard Schuman, 1971. *Makarios: Pragmatism v. Idealism*, Abelard Schuman, 1974.
C. M. Woodhouse: *The Story of Modern Greece*, Faber, 1968.
S. G. Xydis: *Cyprus: The Reluctant Republic*, Mouton, The Hague, 1973. *Cyprus: Conflict and Conciliation, 1954-1958*, Ohio State University Press, 1967.
A. E. Xydis: *Makarios and his Allies*, (in Greek), Athens, 1972.

OFFICIAL PUBLICATIONS

(i) *Cyprus*, H.M.S.O., Cmnd. 1093, 1960.
(ii) Report from the Select Committee on Cyprus, Session 1975-76, H.M.S.O., 8th April 1976.
(iii) *Constitutional Proposals for Cyprus*, H.M.S.O., Cmnd. 42, December 1956.
(iv) Report of the United Nations Mediator on Cyprus to the Secretary-General, printed by the Public Information Office, Cyprus, 1965.
(v) Parliamentary Debates (Hansard), House of Lords, Official Report, H.M.S.O. Nos. 85-86, 14th June 1976.
(vi) *Cyprus Bulletin*, P.I.O.

UNOFFICIAL PUBLICATIONS

(i) *Cyprus Today*.
(ii) *News Week*.
(iii) *Economist*.
(iv) *Quarterly Economic Review*.
(v) *New Statesman*.
(vi) *The Times; The Guardian; The Sun; The Daily Telegraph;*

Washington Post; International Herald Tribune, etc.

Appendices

Letter to Prime Minister Inonu, from President Johnson, dated June 5th, 1964.

Dear Mr. Prime Minister,

I am gravely concerned by the information which I have had through Ambassador Hare from you and your Foreign Minister that the Turkish Government is contemplating a decision to intervene by military force to occupy a portion of Cyprus. I wish to emphasize in the fullest friendship and frankness that I do not consider that such a course of action by Turkey fraught with such far reaching consequences, is consistent with the commitment of your Government to consult fully in advance with United States. Ambassador Hare has indicated that you postponed your decision for a few hours in order to obtain my views. I put to you personally whether you really believe that it is appropriate for your Government, in effect, to present an ultimatum to an ally who has demonstrated such staunch support over the years as has the United States for Turkey. I must, therefore, first urge you to accept the responsibility for complete consultation with the United States before any such action is taken.

It is my impression that you believe that such intervention by Turkey is permissible under the provisions of the Treaty of Guarantee of 1960. I must call your attention, however, to our understanding that the proposed intervention by Turkey would be for the purpose of supporting an attempt by Turkish Cypriot leaders to partition the island, a solution which is specifically excluded by the Treaty of Guarantee. Further, that

Treaty requires consultation among the guarantor powers. It is the view of the United States that the possiblilities of such consultation have by no means been exhausted in this situation and that, therefore, the reservation of the right to take unilateral action is not yet applicable.

I must call your attention also, Mr. Prime Minister, to the obligations of N.A.T.O. There can be no question in your mind that a Turkish intervention in Cyprus would lead to a military engagement between Turkish and Greek forces. Secretary of State Rusk, declared at the recent meeting of the ministerial council for N.A.T.O. in the Hague that war between Turkey and Greece must be considered as 'literally unthinkable'. Adhesion to N.A.T.O. in its very essence, means that N.A.T.O. countries will not wage war on each other. Germany and France have buried centuries of animosity in becoming N.A.T.O. allies; nothing less can be expected from Greece and Turkey. Furthermore, a military intervention in Cyprus by Turkey could lead to direct involvement by the Soviet Union. I hope you will understand that your N.A.T.O. allies have not had a chance to consider whether they have an obligation to protect Turkey against the Soviet Union if Turkey takes a step which results in Soviet intervention without the full consent and understanding of its N.A.T.O. allies.

Further, Mr. Prime Minister, I am concerned about the obligations of Turkey as a member of the United Nations. The United Nations has provided forces on the island to keep the peace. Their task has been difficult but, during the past several weeks, they have been progressively successful in reducing the incidents of violence on that island. The United Nations Mediator has not yet completed his work. I have no doubt that the general membership of the United Nations would react in the strongest terms to unilateral action by Turkey which would defy the efforts of the United Nations and destroy any prospect that the United Nations could assist in obtaining a reasonable and peaceful settlement of this difficult problem.

I wish also, Mr. Prime Minister, to call your attention to the bilateral agreement between the United States and Turkey in the field of military assistance. Under Article IV of the agreement with Turkey of July 1947, your Government is required to obtain United States consent for the use of military assistance for purposes other than those for which such assistance was furnished. Your Government has on several occasions acknowledged to the United States that you fully understand this condition. I must tell you in all candour that the United States cannot agree to the use of any United State supplied military equipment for a Turkish intervention in Cyprus under present circumstances.

Moving to the practical results of the contemplated Turkish move, I feel obligated to call to your attention in the most friendly fashion that such a Turkish move could lead to the slaughter of tens of thousands of Turkish Cypriots on the island of Cyprus. Such an action on your part would unleash the furies and there is no way by which military action on your part could be sufficiently effective to prevent wholesale destruction of many of those whom you are trying to protect. The presence of United Nations forces could not prevent such a catastrophe.

You may consider that what I have said is much too severe and that we are disregardful of Turkish interests in the Cyprus situation. I should like to assure you that this is not the case. We have exerted ourselves both publicly and privately to assure the safety of Turkish Cypriots and to insist that a final solution of the Cyprus problem should rest upon the consent of the parties most directly concerned. It is possible that you feel in Ankara that the United States has not been sufficiently active in your behalf. But surely you know that our policy has caused the liveliest resentments in Athens (where demonstrations have been aimed against us) and has led to a basic alienation between the United States and Archbishop Makarios. As I said to your Foreign Minister in our conversation just a few weeks ago, we value very highly our relations with Turkey. We have considered you as a great ally with fundamental common interests. Your security and prosperity have been a deep concern of the American people and we have expressed that concern in the most practical terms. You and we have fought together to resist the ambitions of the communist world revolution. This solidarity has meant a great deal to us and I would hope that it means a great deal to your Government, and to your people. We have no intention of lending any support to any solution of Cyprus which endangers the Turkish Cypriot community. We have not been able to find a final solution because this is, admittedly, one of the most complex problems on earth. But I wish to assure you that we have been deeply concerned about the interests of Turkey and of the Turkish Cypriots and will remain so.

Finally, Mr. Prime Minister, I must tell you that you have posed the gravest issues of war and peace. These are issues which go beyond the bilateral relations between Turkey and the United States. They not only will certainly involve war between Turkey and Greece, but could involve wider hostilities because of the unpredictable consequences which a unilateral intervention in Cyprus could produce. You have your responsibilities as Chief of the Government of Turkey; I also have mine as President of the United States. I must, therefore, inform you in the deepest friendship that unless I can have your assurance that you will not take such action without further and fullest consultation, I cannot accept your injunction to Ambassador Hare of secrecy and must immediately ask for emergency meetings of the N.A.T.O. Council and of the United Nations Security Council.

I wish it were possible for us to have a personal discussion of this situation. Unfortunately, because of the special circumstances of our present constitutional position, I am not able to leave the United States. If you could come here for a full discussion I would welcome it. I do feel that you and I carry a very heavy responsibility for the general peace and for the possibilities of a sane and peaceful resolution of the Cyprus problem. I ask you, therefore, to delay any decisions which you and your colleagues might have in mind until you and I have had the fullest and frankest consultation.

      Sincerely,
LYNDON B. JOHNSON

APPENDIX II

U.N. SECURITY COUNCIL RESOLUTION 33 OF 20th JULY, 1974

1. Calls upon all States to respect the sovereignty, independence and territorial integrity of Cyprus;

2. Calls upon all parties to the present fighting as a first step to cease all firing and requests all States to exercise the utmost restraint and to refrain from any action which might further aggravate the situation;

3. Demands an immediate end to foreign military intervention in the Republic of Cyprus that is in contravention of operative paragraph 1;

4. Requests the withdrawal without delay from the Republic of Cyprus of foreign military personnel present otherwise than under the authority of International Agreements, including those whose withdrawal was requested by the President of the Republic of Cyprus, Archbishop Makarios, in his letter of 2nd July, 1974;

5. Calls upon Greece, Turkey and the United Kingdom of Great Britain and Northern Ireland to enter into negotiations without delay for the restoration of peace in the area and constitutional government in Cyprus and to keep the Secretary-General informed;

6. Calls upon all parties to co-operate fully with U.N.F.I.C.Y.P. to enable it to carry out its mandate;

7. Decides to keep the situation under constant review and asks the Secretary-General to report as appropriate with a view of adopting further measures in order to ensure that peaceful conditions are restored as soon as possible.

APPENDIX III

GENEVA DECLARATION SIGNED ON 30th JULY, 1974

1. The Foreign Ministers of Greece, Turkey and the United Kingdom held negotiations in Geneva from 25th to 30th July, 1974. They recognised the importance of setting in train, as a matter of urgency, measures to adjust and to regularise within a reasonable period of time the situation in the Republic of Cyprus on a lasting basis, having regard to the international agreement signed at Nicosia on 16th August 1960, and to resolution 353 of the Security Council of the United Nations. They were, however, agreed on the need to decide first on certain immediate measures.
2. The three Foreign Ministers declared that in order to stabilise the situation, the areas in the Republic of Cyprus controlled by opposing armed forces on 30th July, 1974, at 22.00 hours Geneva time should not be extended. They called on all forces, including irregular forces, to desist from all offensive or hostile activities.
4. The three Foreign Ministers, reaffirming that resolution 353 of the Security Council should be implemented in the shortest possible time, agreed that within the framework of a just and lasting solution acceptable to all parties concerned and as peace, security and mutual confidence are established in the Republic of Cyprus, measures should be elaborated which will lead to the timely and phased reduction of the number of armed forces and the amounts of armaments, ammunitions and other war material in the Republic of Cyprus.

Deeply conscious of their responsibilities as regards the maintenance of the independence, territorial and security of the Republic of Cyprus, the three Foreign Ministers agreed that negotiations, as provided for in resolution 353 of the Security Council, should be carried on with the least possible delay to secure (a) the restoration of peace in the area, and (b) the re-establishment of constitutional government in Cyprus.

APPENDIX IV

THE DENKTASH PROPOSALS, GENEVA, 12th AUGUST 1974

(a) The Republic of Cyprus shall be an independent bi-national State.
(b) The Republic shall be composed of two federated states with full control and autonomy within their respective geographical boundaries.
(c) In determining the competence to be left to the Federal Government, the bi-national nature of the State shall be taken into account and the federal competence shall be exercised accordingly.
(d) The area of the Turkish Cypriot Federated State shall cover 34 per centum of the territory of the Republic falling north of a general line starting from the Limnitis-Lefka area in the west and running towards the east, passing through the Turkish controlled part of Nicosia, including the Turkish part of Famagusta and ending at the port of Famagusta.

Pending an agreement on the final Constitutional structure of the Republic, the two autonomous administrations shall take over the full administrative authority within their respective areas as defined above and shall take steps to normalise and stabilise life in the Republic and refrain from acts of violence, harassment and discrimination against each other.

APPENDIX V

PROPOSALS OF MR. CLERIDES AT GENEVA ON 13th AUGUST 1974

1. The constitutional order of Cyprus shall retain its bi-communal character based on the co-existence of the Greek and Turkish communities within the framework of a sovereign, independent and integral Republic.
2. This constitutional order shall, through an appropriate revision and the active co-operation and free consent of the two communities, ensure an enhanced feeling of security for both.

3. The co-existence of the two communities shall be achieved in the context of institutional arrangements regarding an agreed allocation of powers and functions between the Central Government having competence over state affairs and the respective autonomous Communal Administrations exercising their powers on all other matters within areas to be established as in paragraph (5) herein below provided.

4. The structure of the Central Government shall continue to be based on the presidential regime.

5. The Greek and Turkish Communal Administrations shall exercise their powers and functions in areas consisting respectively of the purely Greek and Turkish villages and municipalities. For the purposes of communal administration such villages and municipalities may be grouped together by the respective communal authorities. For the same purpose mixed villages shall come under the communal authorities of the community to which the majority of their inhabitants belong.

6. Legislative authority over the respective Communal Administrations shall be exercised by the Greek and Turkish members of the House of Representatives constituted in separate Councils for this purpose.

13th August, 1974.

APPENDIX VI

SECURITY COUNCIL RESOLUTION 360 (1974)

1. Recalls its formal disapproval of the unilateral military actions undertaken against the Republic of Cyprus;

2. Urges the parties comply with the provisions of the previous resolutions of the Security Council including those concerning the withdrawal without delay from the Republic of Cyprus of foreign military personnel present otherwise than under the authority of international agreements;

3. Urges the parties to resume without delay in an atmosphere of constructive co-operation the negotiations called for in

resolution 353 (1974), whose outcome should not be impeded or prejudged by the acquisition and advantages resulting of military operations;

4. Recalls the Secretary-General to report to it as necessary with a view to possible adoption of further measures designed to promote the restoration of peaceful conditions;

5. Decides to remain permanently seized of the question and to meet at any time to consider measures which may be required in the light of the developing situation.

APPENDIX VII

THE SECURITY COUNCIL RESOLUTION OF 4th MARCH 1975

Following is the full text of the resolution adopted by the U.N. Security Council on Cyprus on 12th March, 1975.

'The Security Council,

having considered the situation in Cyprus in response to the complaint submitted by the Government of the Republic of Cyprus,

having heard the report of the Secretary-General and the statements made by the parties concerned,

deeply concerned at the continuation of the crisis in Cyprus,

recalling its previous resolutions, in particular resolution 365 (1974) of 13 December, 1974, by which it endorsed General Assembly resolution 3212 (XXIX) adopted unanimously on 1 November, 1974,

noting the absence of progress towards the implementation of its resolutions,

1. Calls once more on all States to respect the sovereignty,

independence, territorial integrity and non-alignment of the Republic of Cyprus and urgently requests them, as well as the parties concerned, to refrain from any action which might prejudice that sovereignty, independence, territorial integrity and non-alignment, as well as from any attempt at partition of the island or its unification with any other country.

2. Regrets the unilateral decision of 13 February, 1975, declaring that a part of the Republic of Cyprus would become "a federated Turkish state" as, inter alia, tending to compromise the continuation of negotiations between the representatives of the two communities on an equal footing, the objective of which must continue to be to reach freely a solution providing for a political settlement and the establishment of a mutually acceptable constitutional arrangement, and expresses its concern over all unilateral actions by the parties which have compromised or may compromise the implementation of the relevant United Nations Resolutions.

3. Affirms that the decision referred to in paragraph 2 above does not prejudice the final political settlement of the problem of Cyprus and takes note of the declaration that this was not its intention.

4. Calls for the urgent and effective implementation of all parts and provisions of General Assembly Resolution 3212 (XXIX) endorsed by Security Council Resolution 365 (1974),

5. Considers that new efforts should be undertaken to assist the resumption of the negotiations referred to in paragraph 4 of General Assembly Resolution 3212 (XXIX) between the representatives of the two communities.

6. Requests the Secretary-General accordingly to undertake a new mission of good offices and to that end to convene the parties under new agreed procedures and place himself personally at their disposal, so that the resumption, the intensification and the progress of comprehensive negotiations, carried out in a reciprocal spirit of understanding and of

moderation under his personal auspices and with his direction as appropriate, might thereby be facilitated.

7. Calls on the representatives of the two communities to co-operate closely with the Secretary-General in the discharge of his new mission of good offices and asks them to accord personally a high priority to their negotiations.

8. Calls on all the parties concerned to refrain from any action which might jeopardize the negotiations between the representatives of the two communities and to take steps which will facilitate the creation of the climate necessary for the success of those negotiations,

9. Requests the Secretary-General to keep the Security Council informed of the progress made towards the implementation of Resolution 365 (1974) and of this resolution and to report to it whenever he considers it appropriate and, in any case, before 15 June, 1975.

10. Decides to remain actively seized of the matter.'

APPENDIX VIII

CYPRUS GOVERNMENT PROPOSALS TO THE TURKS

Mr. Glafcos Clerides, President of the House of Representatives, and Greek Cypriot negotiator at the intercommunal talks, in his capacity as Head of the Cyprus Delegation at the United Nations Security Session, disclosed in his statement the proposals he had handed to the Turkish Cypriot side, on 10 February, 1975 setting out the views of the Cyprus Government for a Cyprus settlement.

The proposals are as follows:

The Greek Cypriot representative at the Cyprus talks proposes that the Constitution of the Republic of Cyprus shall be based on the following principles:

1. Cyprus shall be an independant sovereign republic.

2. The Constitution shall be that of a bi-communal multi-regional federal state.

3. The areas to be administered by the Turkish Cypriots may include a substantial area in the north extending on both sides of the Nicosia-Kyrenia axis to the sea.

4. Other areas under Turkish Cypriot administration shall be formed where Turkish Cypriot villages are mainly concentrated.

5. The total extent of areas to be under Turkish Cypriot administration shall correspond approximately to the present ratio of the Greek and Turkish population in the island.

6. Should there be need, for purposes of administration, of a substantial Turkish-Cypriot majority in areas to be under Turkish-Cypriot administration, the Republic will undertake the financial responsibility of the cost of building houses for Turkish Cypriots in Turkish villages, who finally may wish to be settled in areas which will come under Turkish-Cypriot administration.

7. The Central Government of the Federal State shall have substantial powers.

8. The legal status of Greek-Cypriots, who will be living in areas under Turkish-Cypriot administration, and that of Turkish-Cypriots, who will live in areas under Greek-Cypriot administration, shall be defined and entrenched.

9. Human rights shall be entrenched in the Constitution, including the right of freedom of movement throughout the island, the existing rights of property and the right to acquire, own, possess, use and enjoy property in any area or place in Cyprus.

The proposals do not affect the provisions of resolution 3212 of the United Nations General Assembly and, in particular, those regarding the speedy withdrawal of all foreign armed forces from Cyprus and the return of all refugees to their homes, which should be implemented.

NOTE: These proposals do not deal with the question of guarantees, which should be effective and wide.

APPENDIX IX

GENERAL PRINCIPLES CONCERNING THE ESTABLISHMENT OF A FEDERAL REPUBLIC IN CYPRUS—TURKISH PROPOSALS

1. Cyprus shall be a Federal Republic composed of two Federated States one in the North for the Turkish national community and one in the South for the Greek national community.

2. The Federal Republic shall be independent, sovereign and territorially integral.

3. The sovereignty shall continue to be shared equally by the two national communities as co-founders of the Republic.

4. The Federal Republic shall be secular. Religion shall be kept strictly out of politics in Federal and Federated affairs.

5. Equality of power and status of and non-discrimination between the two Federated States shall be ensured. Any of the States can in no way overpower, dominate, overrun or interfere with the other in political, juridical, military, economic or other fields.

The Federal Government can in no case abolish, engage in any warlike activity against, or otherwise interfere with, any of the Federated States.

6. Each Federated State shall be free to maintain and regulate its own Constitutional structure and take all such measures relating to its administration as may be necessary.

7. Under no circumstances shall Cyprus, in whole or in part, be united with any other State. Unilateral declaration of independence by any of the Federated States shall be prohibited.

8. The Federal Republic of Cyprus shall henceforth follow a policy of friendship with Turkey and Greece in addition to promoting good neighbourly relations with countries in the region and shall pursue a policy of non-alignment.

9. All necessary measures shall be taken to prevent the Island of Cyprus from becoming involved, directly or indirectly, in any activity endangering the peace and security of the region.

10. Each Federated State shall ensure respect for Human Rights within its respective territory.

11. Laws and all other measures, such as administrative, economic, social etc., of the Federal Government shall not discriminate against either of the two Federated States or of the two national communities.

12. All kinds of hostile activities of the two States against each other in both the internal and international spheres shall be excluded, while every effort shall be made to enhance peaceful coexistence, reconciliation and, co-operation between the two national communities. Likewise any activity tending to foment enmity, hatred and ill-feelings between the two national communities shall be prohibited.

13. Concurrently with the building up of mutual confidence and trust and subject to security needs of the Federated States, the overall effort of the two States shall be directed towards normalization of the relations between the two national

communities in all respects.

14. The question of proprietary rights and claims arising therefrom or relating thereto, as well as any other claims, shall be settled by mutual agreement between the parties concerned, in conjunction with the question of compensation and other related matter, in such a manner as not to obstruct the setting up of the proposed Federal Republic.

APPENDIX X

POPULATION SINCE THE MIDDLE AGES

Year	Total estimated population	Remarks
Early 14th century	400,000	Estimate based on 1491 figures.
1491	168,000	Venetian count in Mas Latrie, vol. 111, 147, 700, about 20,000 persons not included.
1540	217,000	Venetian count (Attar), 197,000, about 20,000 persons not included.
1571	290,000	Turkish count, 85,000 Christian taxpayers plus dependents, plus 20,000 Turks.
1641	130,000	Turkish count, 25,000 taxpayers, plus dependents, plus Turks.
1670	100,000	Turkish count, 15,000 taxpayers, plus dependents, plus Turks.
1745	85,000	Turkish count, 12,000 taxpayers, plus dependents and 4,000 Turkish families.
1767	80,000	Turkish count, of villages only approximately 10,000 taxpayers, plus dependents and 6,000 Turkish families.
1777	100,000	Estimate of Kyprianos (37,000 Christians, 47,000 Moslems)—Christians probably understated.
1821	110,000	Estimate of Trikoupi (21,000 each

		Christians and Moslems, plus dependents).
1881	186,000	First census under British occupation (140,000 Christians, 45,500 Moslems).
1911	274,000	Fourth census (218,000 Christians, 54,000 Moslems).
1946	450,000	Seventh census (369,500 Christians, 80,500 Moslems).
1959	561,000	Cyprus: Colonial Report, 1959, p. 16. Greek Cypriots (78.8 percent) and Turkish Cypriots (17.5 percent): other minorities.

'Cyprus: Census of Population and Agriculture 1946', published on behalf of the Government of Cyprus by the Crown Agents for the Colonies, 1949.

APPENDIX XI

CYPRUS IN HISTORY

6th millenium B.C. — Earliest neolithic settlements at Khirokitis, Troulli, Erimi, Kalavasos.

3rd millenium B.C. — First appearance of copper.

2nd millenium B.C. — Arrival of Mycenaean Greeks and Achaeans from Peloponnese, Greece; spreading of their culture, Hellenisation.

— City-kingdoms are established throughout Cyprus.

8th-5th cent. B.C. — Vicissitudes of the city-kingdoms with foreign powers from the East and Africa; the Assyrians (8th-6th cent.), the Egyptians (560-540 B.C.), the Persians (540-132 B.C.).

6th cent. B.C.	— Stassinos, the poet of 'Cypria Epica.' — The Athenian statesman Solon visits the island and the city of Soli is named after him.
499 B.C.	— Onesilos, King of Salamis. — Cyprus joins the Ionian Revolt.
449 B.C.	— Kimon, the Athenian general, is killed at Kition.
411-374 B.C.	— Evagoras I, King of Salamis, makes Cyprus one of the leading political and cultural centres of the Greek world; the Athenian orator Isocrates proposes Evagoras as the leader of Hellenism.
330 B.C.	— The city-kingdoms of Cyprus welcome Alexander the Great and participate in his enterprises. — Zeno of Kition (340-264 B.C.), the founder of the stoic philosophy.
323-30 B.C.	— Cyprus is part of the Ptolemaic Empire.
30-330 A.D.	— Cyprus is a province of the Roman Empire. — 1st Cent. A.D.: Christianity is introduced by St. Paul and St. Barnabas—the latter is considered to be the founder of the Church of Cyprus.
330-1191 A.D.	— Cyprus a province of the Byzantine Empire.
1191-1571 A.D.	— Cyprus under the Crusaders; Richard I of England, the Lionheart (1191), the Order of the Knight Templars (1191),

	the French Lusignans (1192-1489), the Venetians (1489-1571).
1571-1878 A.D.	— Cyprus under Ottoman occupation.
1878-1960	— Cyprus under British occupation. 1878-1914: Cyprus leased by Turkey to the British. 1914: Cyprus annexed by Britain. 1923: Turkey relinquishes all rights on Cyprus under the Treaty of Lausanne. 1925: Cyprus declared a Crown Colony. 1931: Greek Cypriot popular rising in favour of Union with Greece. 1950: In a nation-wide plebiscite the Greek Cypriots vote almost unanimously for Union with Greece. 1954: First Greek appeal to U.N.O. for self-determination. 1955-59: Liberation Struggle. 1959: Zurich-London Agreements. 1960: Cyprus declared an independent State and member of U.N.O., joins British Commonwealth and the Council for Europe. Her sovereignty and territorial integrity guaranteed by Britain, Turkey and Greece (Treaty of Guarantee 1960).
1963	— President Makarios submits moderate proposals for democratic revision of the Constitution. Dec. 21, 22: Turkish insurrection.
1964	— March 4, 13: U.N. Security Council 1st and 2nd Resolutions. March 27: U.N. Peace-keeping Force sent to Cyprus. June 20: U.N. Security Council 3rd Resolution.

August 7, 8, 9: Turkish air attacks on Cyprus.
August 9: U.N. Security Council Emergency Resolution.
August 11: U.N. Security Council Concensus.
September 25: U.N. Security Council 4th Resolution.
December 18: U.N. Security Council 5th Resolution.

1965 — March 19: U.N. Security Council 7th Resolution.

1967
— April 21: The coup in Greece.
— November 29: Agreement was reached between Greece and Turkey to withdraw from Cyprus all their forces except those contingents provided by the Zurich-London agreements.

1968
— January 12: Archbishop Makarios speaks of 'that which is desirable is not always feasible'.
— February 25: Presidential Elections result in a renewal of Makarios' mandate by a 96.4 percent majority.
— June 24: The Intercommunal talks start.

1970 — March 8: The helicopter assassination attempt. Makarios survives.

1971 — July 2: Makarios visits Moscow.

1973 — March 13: The three Bishops of Cyprus proclaimed the unfrocking of Archbishop Makarios for non-compliance

with their demand to abandon his political office or resign as Archbishop.
— July 14: A Major Ecclesiastical Synod —the Patriarchs of Alexandria and Antioch and fourteen Bishops from three Patriarchates—dethrone and unfrock the three Cypriot Bishops and proclaim new elections to fill their places.

1974

— January 28: General George Grivas dies in Limassol.
— July 2: Makarios writes a letter to General Ghizikis demanding the withdrawal of the Greek officers from the National Guard. Makarios accuses members of the Junta and Greek C.I.A. of financing and controlling the activities of E.O.K.A.-B. and plotting to overthrow him.
— July 15: Military coup in Cyprus. Nicos Sampson named President.
— July 16: President Makarios leaves Cyprus through the British Base at Akrotiri and spends the night in Malta.
— July 17: President Makarios arrives in London.
— July 18: President Makarios flies to New York to address U.N. where he was accepted as the legitimate President of Cyprus.
— July 20: Turkey invades Cyprus under the pretext of the Treaty of Guarantee for the safety of the Turkish Cypriots. The Turkish Prime Minister, Mr. B. Ecevit, declares: 'We are not bringing war but peace to Cyprus, to Greek as

well as to Turkish Cypriots'.
— July 23: Collapse of Junta in Greece. Constantine Karamanlis returns to Athens. Nicos Sampson resigns and Glafcos Clerides is sworn in as President.
— July 24: Constantine Karamanlis is sworn in as Prime Minister of Greece.
— July 25-30: Geneva negotiations, Geneva Declaration signed.
— August 8-14: Geneva negotiations, second phase, gunboat diplomacy adopted by Turkey.
— August 14: U.N. Security Council Resolution 357.
— August 15: U.N. Security Council Resolution 358 and 359.
— August 16: U.N. Security Council Resolution 360.
— August 30: Assassination attempt against Dr. Vassos Lyssarides, leader of E.D.E.K.
— September 6: Clerides and Denktash meet for first time since Geneva breakdown.
— September 11: Second meeting between Clerides and Denktash with U.N. special envoy present.
— September 17: Mr. Bulent Ecevit resigns as Prime Minister.
— September 24: U.S. House of Representatives votes to cut off military aid to Turkey unless there is 'substantial progress' towards agreement on the removal of all foreign troops from Cyprus.
— September 29: About 60,000 Greek Cypriots demonstrate in Limassol for

return of President Makarios who was staying at the Grosvenor House Hotel, London.
— September 30: Mr. Demirel is asked to form a Government in Turkey.
— October 1: President Makarios speaks at U.N. General Assembly, rejecting geographical federation of the island.
— October 4: Acting President Clerides refers publicly for the first time to Archbishop Makarios as the President.
— October 28: Exchange of prisoners completed but large numbers remain missing.
— November 13: President Makarios meets Dr. Kissinger in Washington.
— November 20: Clerides flies to London to see the Archbishop and the British Government.
— November 29: President Makarios arrives in Athens.
— December 5: The E.O.K.A.-B. guerrilla movement, in a 10-point manifesto, attacks President Makarios and declares it will accept his return if he gives up the Presidency and restricts himself to church affairs.
— December 7: More than 200,000 Greek Cypriots welcome President Makarios on his return to Cyprus after nearly five months' exile.

1975

— January 2: Mr. Bulent Ecevit arrives in Cyprus for a five-day visit.
— January 3: Mr. Ecevit says Turkey no longer recognises Archbishop Makarios as President of Cyprus.
— January 14: President Makarios an-

nounces the formation of a new nine-man Cabinet. (five were members of the ousted Makarios cabinet).
— January 15: The British Foreign Office announces that the Turkish Cypriot refugees will be allowed to leave the Akrotiri Base for Turkey.
— January 15: Brigadier Joannides, the former Greek Junta leader, is arrested and imprisoned.
— February 2: Turkish Cypriot Airways begin flying scheduled passenger services between the Turkish mainland and a newly-built airport at Tymbou (Ercan).
— February 9: President Makarios convenes a special meeting of the National Council for a briefing on the proposals to be submitted to Mr. Denktash.
— February 10: Clerides submits the Proposals based on the concept of a 'multi-regional' federation.
— February 13: The Turkish Cypriot authorities declare the Turkish-held North of Cyprus a 'Secular and Federated State'.
— March 7: After three hours of talks in Brussels, Dr. Kissinger and Mr. Bitsios are reported to be guardedly optimistic about the Cyprus situation.
— March 12: After three weeks of intense negotiations the intercommunal talks were to start soon under the chairmanship of the U.N. Secretary-General, Dr. Kurt Waldheim.
— March 31: Demirel becomes Prime Minister of Turkey.
— April 28: The Vienna Talks begin.

— July 2: Turkish colonists arrive in the north part of the island.
— August 1: Agreement has been reached at the Vienna Talks for 9,000 Turkish Cypriots to cross the 'Attila Line' and join their compatriots in the north of Cyprus. The 10,000 Greek Cypriots in the northern part of the island would be allowed to remain there and the 800 Greek Cypriots expelled at the end of June would be allowed to return to their homes.
— September 10: The intercommunal talks in New York end because the Turkish Cypriots failed to honour their promise to submit written proposals.
— September 23: President Makarios flies to New York to address the U.N. General Assembly.
— November 12: Mr. Bitsios meets Mr. Chaglayangil in Brussels. Dr. Kissinger says that Greece and Turkey are 'close to resolving' differences.
— November 14: Mr. G. Tzounis, Director-General of the Greek Foreign Ministry, flies to Nicosia to brief Makarios and Clerides on the Brussels talks of 12th November 1975.

1976

— January 5: A delegation of six British parliamentarians begin a five-day fact-finding visit to Cyprus.
— January 14: Clerides announces his resignation from the post of negotiator for the Greek Cypriot side.
— January 17: Clerides withdraws his resignation following appeals from Greek Premiere Karamanlis, U.N.

Secretary-General, Dr. Waldheim and parliamentary colleagues.
— February 17: Intercommunal talks held in Vienna under the chairmanship of Dr. Waldheim. Denktash and Clerides reached a secret agreement whereby the Greek Cypriots were to produce fresh proposals by 23rd March, which were to be countered with Turkish Cypriot proposals within a period of ten days.
— March 16: Nicos Sampson, the eight-day self-proclaimed 'president' of Cyprus was arrested and is still being held in custody on charges of carrying out or aiding warlike activities.
— April 8: Report from the Select Committee on Cyprus. The gist of the Report is that Britain acted both illegally and immorally not to have prevented the Turkish invasion of Cyprus in 1974.
— April 9: Denktash revealed the secret agreement and rejected the Greek Cypriot proposals. Clerides resigned on 9th April as the Greek Cypriot negotiator.
— April 17: The Turkish Cypriot side submitted their proposals.
— May 30: President Makarios rejected the latest Turkish Cypriot proposals as 'totally unreasonable and completely unacceptable'.
— June 20: By now there has been no progress at all. As mentioned already the Greek Cypriot negotiator, Mr. Glafcos Clerides, had been forced to resign; he has been succeeded by Mr.

Tassos Papodopoulos; the intercommunal talks have been suspended; the Greek Cypriots' proposals have been rejected; the Turkish Cypriots' proposals have also been rejected. What next? (i) U.N. initiative? (ii) Lord Caradon's suggestion? (iii) E.E.C. initiative? (iv) Commonwealth mediation? (v) the two super-powers' joint action? etc.